The Informal Economy and Islamic Finance

The characteristics, nature, determinants, and size of the informal economy differ from country to country. While much research has been carried out in the context of advanced economies, less attention has been given to developing countries, especially those in the Organisation of Islamic Cooperation (OIC) nations.

This is one of the first books to investigate Islamic finance's stance on the informal economy and to discuss it from an OIC perspective. It covers the various definitions, historical development, types, and determining factors behind the shadow economy and the reasons for people's preference to join and stay in the informal economy. Similarly, different theories are discussed in detail, thus providing a deeper understanding of the subject matter.

The book examines the indicators of the informal sector, such as unemployment, regulation, and taxation, and the effect of financial development and the role of financial inclusion in informal economy in the case of OIC countries compared to non-OIC countries. It defines the main features of the informal economy and discusses their implications for policy formation and implementation. Additionally, the author provides guidance on Islamic finance's role in the informal economy and offers policy recommendations in order to bring more people into the formal economy.

The book presents deep and specialist knowledge on the shadow economy as well as facts and figures pertaining to OIC countries, and, as such, will open the door for future research in this important but understudied field, especially from an Islamic finance angle. It can be used as a comprehensive guide for students, academics, and researchers of Islamic studies, development economics, political economy, public policy, law, sociology, and anthropology.

Shabeer Khan, PhD, is an assistant professor in the Department of Islamic Economics and Finance at Sakarya University, Turkey. He is a Shariah board member of the Tayyib Advisory UAE and a Shariah consultant to KalPay Financial Services, Pakistan, and Muawin, Pakistan. Moreover, he is also a trainer and consultant with ifintel in Malaysia.

Islamic Business and Finance Series
Series Editor: Ishaq Bhatti

There is an increasing need for western politicians, financiers, bankers, and indeed the western business community in general to have access to high quality and authoritative texts on Islamic financial and business practices. Drawing on expertise from across the Islamic world, this new series will provide carefully chosen and focused monographs and collections, each authored/edited by an expert in their respective field all over the world.

The series will be pitched at a level to appeal to middle and senior management in both the western and the Islamic business communities. For the manager with a western background the series will provide detailed and up-to-date briefings on important topics; for the academics, postgraduates, business communities, manager with western and an Islamic background the series will provide a guide to best practice in business in Islamic communities around the world, including Muslim minorities in the west and majorities in the rest of the world.

Islamic Capital Markets
The Structure, Formation and Management of Sukuk
Imam Uddin, Rabia Sabri, M. Ishaq Bhatti, Muhammad Omer Rafique and Muhammad AsadUllah

Institutional Islamic Economics and Finance
Edited by Ahsan Shafiq

Islamic Finance in the Financial Markets of Europe, Asia and America
Faiza Ismail

The Informal Economy and Islamic Finance
The Case of Organisation of Islamic Cooperation Countries
Shabeer Khan

For more information about this series, please visit: www.routledge.com/Islamic-Business-and-Finance-Series/book-series/ISLAMICFINANCE

The Informal Economy and Islamic Finance

The Case of Organisation of Islamic Cooperation Countries

Shabeer Khan

LONDON AND NEW YORK

First published 2023
by Routledge
4 Park Square, Milton Park, Abingdon, Oxon OX14 4RN

and by Routledge
605 Third Avenue, New York, NY 10158

Routledge is an imprint of the Taylor & Francis Group, an informa business

© 2023 Shabeer Khan

The right of Shabeer Khan to be identified as author of this work has been asserted in accordance with sections 77 and 78 of the Copyright, Designs and Patents Act 1988.

All rights reserved. No part of this book may be reprinted or reproduced or utilised in any form or by any electronic, mechanical, or other means, now known or hereafter invented, including photocopying and recording, or in any information storage or retrieval system, without permission in writing from the publishers.

Trademark notice: Product or corporate names may be trademarks or registered trademarks, and are used only for identification and explanation without intent to infringe.

British Library Cataloguing-in-Publication Data
A catalogue record for this book is available from the British Library

Library of Congress Cataloging-in-Publication Data
Names: Khan, Shabeer, author.
Title: The informal economy and Islamic finance : the case of organisation of Islamic cooperation countries / Shabeer Khan.
Description: Abingdon, Oxon ; New York, NY : Routledge, 2023. | Series: Islamic business and finance | Includes bibliographical references and index.
Identifiers: LCCN 2022030067 (print) | LCCN 2022030068 (ebook) | ISBN 9781032360324 (hbk) | ISBN 9781032360348 (pbk) | ISBN 9781003329954 (ebk)
Subjects: LCSH: Economics—Islamic countries. | Finance—Islamic countries. | Banks and banking—Islamic countries. | Islamic countries—Economic policy.
Classification: LCC HB126.4 .K48 2023 (print) | LCC HB126.4 (ebook) | DDC 330.917/67—dc23/eng/20220906
LC record available at https://lccn.loc.gov/2022030067
LC ebook record available at https://lccn.loc.gov/2022030068

ISBN: 978-1-032-36032-4 (hbk)
ISBN: 978-1-032-36034-8 (pbk)
ISBN: 978-1-003-32995-4 (ebk)

DOI: 10.4324/9781003329954

Typeset in Times New Roman
by Apex CoVantage, LLC

Contents

List of Tables	viii
List of Figures	ix
List of Abbreviations	x

1 Overview of the Shadow Economy   1

1.1 Background of Shadow Economy *1*
1.2 Historical Development of Shadow Economy *2*
1.3 Meaning and Definitions of Shadow Economy *6*
1.4 Measurements of Shadow Economy *9*
1.5 Economic Impacts of Shadow Economy *19*

2 Shadow Economy and Islamic Finance   22

2.1 Islamic Economic System and Shadow Economy *22*
2.2 Objectives of Shariah vis-à-vis Shadow Economy *22*
*2.3 Shadow Economy, Multiplier and Crowding Out
Effects in Islamic Economy* *23*
2.4 Brief History of Islamic Finance *24*
2.5 Informal Finance and OIC Countries *24*
2.6 Islamic Banking Sector and Shadow Economy *26*
*2.7 Role of Islamic Micro Financial Institutions (IMFI)
in Shadow Economy* *26*
2.8 The Way Forward for Inclusive Micro-Takaful *27*
2.9 Conclusion *28*

3 Main Causal Factors of Shadow Economy   29

3.1 Tax and Social Security Contribution *29*
3.2 Intensity of Regulations *31*
3.3 Public Sector Service *32*
3.4 Official Economy *33*
3.5 Unemployment *33*

vi   *Contents*

4   Empirical Scholarship on Shadow Economy   35

   4.1   Empirical Literature on the Determinants of Shadow Economy   35

   4.2   Empirical Literature on Financial Development and Shadow Economy   38

   4.3   Empirical Literature on Financial Inclusion and Shadow Economy   39

5   Theories of Shadow Economy   42

   5.1   The Dualist School   42

   5.2   The Structuralist/Dependency School   47

   5.3   The Legalist/Neoliberal School   48

   5.4   Complementary Theory   52

   5.5   Voluntarist/Rational Exit Theory   53

   5.6   Illegalist Thought   55

   5.7   Inclusionist Perspective   56

   5.8   The Modern Perspective   57

   5.9   Shadow Economy Theories Application to OIC Countries   59

6   The Model and Empirical Investigation of Shadow Economy   63

   6.1   The Estimating Models   63

     6.1.1   Estimation Equations for the Determinants of Shadow Economy   63

     6.1.2   Estimation Equations for Financial Development Impact on Shadow Economy   65

     6.1.3   Estimation Equations for Financial Inclusion Impact on Shadow Economy   67

   6.2   The Method of Estimations   68

   6.3   Sources of Data and Description of the Variables   73

     6.3.1   Variables   74

   6.4   Conclusion   76

7   Results and Discussion   77

   7.1   Descriptive Statistics   77

   7.2   Correlation Analysis   79

   7.3   Results and Discussion   79

   7.4   Determinants of Shadow Economy With Full Sample and Subsamples   79

     7.4.1   The Effects of Economic Growth on Shadow Economy   83

Contents   vii

7.4.2 *The Effects of Government Expenditure on Shadow Economy   83*
7.4.3 *The Effects of Institutional Quality on Shadow Economy   84*
7.5 *Financial Development and Shadow Economy   84*
7.5.1 *The Effect of Financial Development on Shadow Economy   84*
7.6 *Financial Inclusion and Shadow Economy   86*
7.6.1 *The Effect of Financial Inclusion on Shadow Economy   86*
7.7 *Robustness Checks   101*
7.7.1 *Full Sample and Subsamples   101*
7.7.2 *An Alternative Measure of Institution Variables   101*
7.8 *Conclusion   101*

8   Inferences and Policy Implications   104
8.1 *Policy Implications   105*

Appendices   107
References   119
Index   135

Tables

1.1	Monetary and nonmonetary activities	15
1.2	Sectors of shadow economy by legality and market transaction	15
7.1	Descriptive statistics	78
7.2	Correlation coefficients of variables	80
7.3	Determinants of shadow economy with full sample and subsamples	81
7.4	Financial development and shadow economy with OIC dummy (D1)	82
7.5	Financial development interaction with OIC dummy (D1)	85
7.6	Financial inclusion and shadow economy using proxies of ATMs per 100,000 adults and bank deposit (% of GDP)	88
7.7	Financial inclusion and shadow economy using proxies of bank branches per 100,000 adults and bank credit to bank deposits (%)	90
7.8	Interactive terms	101
7.9	Testing level of significance between OIC and non-OIC countries	101
7.10	Comparative mean of variables	102
A1	Determinants of shadow economy using rule of law	107
A2	Determinants of shadow economy using political stability	108
A3a	Determinants of shadow economy with tax	110
A3b	Interaction of OIC dummy (D1 = 1) with bank deposits to GDP (D1*LBD) and automated teller machines (ATMs) per 100,000 adults (D1*LATM)	111
A4	Interaction of OIC dummy and bank branches per 100,000 adults' interaction (D1*LBB) and bank credit to bank deposits (%) (D1*LBCBD)	113
A5	Interactive term of bank deposits to GDP (%)	114
A6	Interactive term of automated teller machines (ATMs)	
A7	Interactive term of domestic credit to private sector by banks (% of GDP)	115
A8	Descriptive statistics (variables in level form)	116
A9	List of variables	116
A10	List of countries	118

Figures

1.1	Average size of shadow economy (% of GDP) in non-OIC, OIC, LOIC and HOIC	9
1.2	Average size of shadow economy (% of GDP) in full sample	10
1.3	Average size of shadow economy (% of GDP) in non-OIC countries	10
1.4	Average size of shadow economy (% of GDP) in OIC countries	11
1.5	Vicious cycle of shadow economy	12
1.6	Average size of shadow economy (% of GDP) in the World, OIC and non-OIC	13
1.7	Size of shadow economy by years for OIC and non-OIC countries	14
1.8	Potential economy, official economy, and shadow economy	16
1.9	Distribution of shadow economy	17
7.1	Marginal effect of bank deposit on shadow economy	93
7.2	Marginal effect of number of ATMs on shadow economy	93
7.3	Marginal effect of bank branch on shadow economy	95
7.4	Marginal effect of bank credit to bank deposit on shadow economy	95
7.5	Marginal effect of bank deposit on shadow economy in case of full sample	96
7.6	Marginal effect of bank deposit on shadow economy in case of OIC and non-OIC countries	96
7.7	Margin predictive values of bank deposit with respect to shadow economy for OIC and non-OIC countries	97
7.8	Margin predictive values of bank deposit on shadow economy for OIC and non-OIC countries	97
7.9	Association between ATM number and shadow economy in full sample	98
7.10	Association between ATM number and shadow economy in non-OIC countries	98
7.11	Association between ATM number and shadow economy in OIC countries	99
7.12	Association between bank credit to bank deposit and shadow economy in full sample	99
7.13	Association between bank credit to bank deposit and shadow economy in non-OIC countries	100
7.14	Association between bank credit to bank deposit and shadow economy in OIC countries	100

List of Abbreviations

AD	Aggregate Demand
AR	Autoregressive
ARDL	Autoregressive Distributed Lag
COMCEC	The Standing Committee for Economic and Commercial Cooperation of the Organisation of the Islamic Cooperation
EU	Europe Union
FE	Fixed Effect
GCC	Gulf Cooperation Council
GDP	Gross Domestic Product
GMM	Generalized Method of Movements
GNP	Gross National Product
HOIC	High Income OIC Countries
IDB	Islamic Development Bank
IFC	International Finance Corporation
IFIs	Islamic Financial Institutions
ILO	International Labor Organisation
IMF	International Monetary Fund
IMFI	Islamic Micro Financial Institutions
ISB	Islamic Social Business
LOIC	Low Income OIC Countries
MIMIC	Multiple Indicator, Multiple Cause Model
MMSEs	Medium, Micro, and Small Enterprises
MPC	Marginal Propensity to Consume
OECD	Organisation for Economic Co-operation and Development
OIC	Organisation of Islamic Cooperation
OLS	Ordinary Least Square
SDGs	Sustainable Development Goals
SE	Shadow Economy
SMEs	Small and Medium-sized Enterprises
UN	United Nations
VAR	Vector Autoregressive
IV	Instrumental Variable
WHF	World Heritage Foundation

WB	World Bank
WDI	World Development Indicators
WGI	World Governance Indicators
WIEGO	Women in Informal Employment Globalizing and Organizing
WTO	World Trade Organisation

1 Overview of the Shadow Economy

This chapter introduces the idea of shadow economy. There is not only debate in the literature regarding the methods of estimation of shadow economy but also a concern about its proper definition. Scholars disagree on a unified definition. The reason behind such disagreement is the fact that shadow economy is hidden and not directly observable. In recent decades, researchers have given considerable attention to the shadow economy in advanced and transition countries. But there are few studies on developing economies, while studies on OIC member countries are rare. In order to have a deeper understanding of shadow economy, we first provide the background of shadow economy, its historical development, meaning and definitions, measurements, and its economic impact. This chapter covers all these concepts.

1.1 Background of Shadow Economy

At the beginning of the twentieth century, the notion of shadow economy was not discussed by the economists in academic circles, and it had no room in the economic activities of a country. However, in the scholarship of anthropologists and sociologists, such activities did exist and were discussed extensively in their literature. Anthropologist Keith Hart (1971, 1973) was the first person who coined the term "informal sector" in 1971 while studying the economy of Ghana (Igudia, 2014; Bangasser, 2000; Gërxhani, 2004 and Dotti et al., 2015). Similarly, considerable credit also goes to the International Labor Organization (ILO) in an extended study about Kenya in 1972 where shadow economy was presented more precisely to researchers and economists with the title of "informal sector" (Gërxhani, 2004; Igudia, 2014; Bangasser, 2000; Swaminathan, 1991 and ILO, 1972). A dominant scholar in this area, Schneider (1986: p. 643), defines shadow economy as "all economic activities that add value to the economy and which are required to be taken into account in national income of a country but currently are absent from national accounting".

Today, shadow economy is a global reality, and it is an important issue for a majority of the countries with an increasing attention toward its significant impact on macroeconomic fundamentals of the official economy (Schneider and Enste, 2000; Voicu, 2012 and Trebicka, 2014). In one form or another, it

DOI: 10.4324/9781003329954-1

2 Overview of the Shadow Economy

exists everywhere and will continue to exist with persistent characteristics in all countries (Blackburn et al., 2012). Great interest has been shown by researchers, economists, and politicians regarding shadow economy for the last two decades. The reason behind such interest is that it has important implications for the formal economy. Taking into consideration the 2008 financial crisis, studying shadow economy is crucial for governments, as its presence decreases government revenue. Consequently, governments have less resources to handle crises. Relative to formal economy, the size of shadow economy is large in many developing nations. From an economic and social policy perspective, it is essential for policy makers to know the accurate size of the economy to develop proper economic policies at regional and country levels (Schneider and Enste, 2000 and González-Fernández and González-Velasco, 2015).

Ignoring shadow economy and only relying on official economy is not a realistic approach, and it may create three main problems in terms of social and economic conditions of households, countries, and individuals. First, shadow economic activities are not subject to taxation, which results in governments losing huge tax revenue. Second, informal economy creates an unfair relationship between government and individuals because it shows people's unhappiness with the government services in response to their input and contribution to the economy. Therefore, they tend to join shadow economy to balance their satisfaction and utilities. Hence, the existence of shadow economy will decrease government revenue, and government will be unable to finance public goods and services. Third, government policies will be excessive and expansionary, since the people who are working in the shadow economy are paid for the goods and services they are supplying, while officially they are considered unemployed (Frey and Schneider, 2000).

1.2 Historical Development of Shadow Economy

The concept of shadow economy emerged in the last half of the twentieth century. There were two main studies that introduced the concept of "informal sector". The first study was conducted by Keith Hart in 1971, which investigated the economy of Ghana. Second, the International Labor Organization, in 1972, studied the economy of Kenya and also used the term "informal sector" (Hart, 1970, 1973 and ILO, 1972). Both studies debated the same phenomena, even though both studies were different regarding definition and description. Similarly, the discussion regarding informal sector can also be traced back to the second half of twentieth century when Furnivall (1939) discussed informal sector in his book *Netherlands India: A Study of Plural Economy*. Similarly, in his famous book *The Theory of Economic Growth*, Lewis (1955) discussed informal sector.

According to O'Conner (1983), the features of shadow economy have a close connection with pre-capitalist civilizations, too, where informal work was the only source of income or livelihood for all societies prior to the industrial revolution. In his famous book *Economic Development with Unlimited Supplies of Labour*, Lewis (1954) accepted that there were an enormous number of working

Overview of the Shadow Economy 3

people in developing economies and pointed out that economic development and growth was the solution to employing such a massive supply of labor in official sector. The scholars who support this view argue that as the economy grew and developed, the traditional segment (informal sector), which consists of small producers and sellers, uncertain employment, and petty suppliers, will disappear and this old and traditional segment (informal sector) will merged into the present industrial sector (formal sector) of the economy. Therefore, economic development is a source of reduction in a traditional economy[1] (Chen et al., 2002). According to Willman-Navarro (2008), the concept of informal sector can also be found in the book *Capital* by Karl Marx, where he states that as the capitalist production[2] grows and continues to progress, the commodity production[3] starts shrinking and disappearing. The scholars who agree with this proposition hold a position that the traditional sector (informal sector) will disappear as the capitalist sector (official sector) matures. Similarly, an accelerated growth model also considers that with large-scale industrialization, workers from the unproductive sector (informal sector) of the economy would shift to the industrialized sector of the economy.

To summarize, all the aforementioned three models – that is, Lewis, Marx, and accelerated models – agree that the traditional sector would either be eliminated or would be absorbed by modern industrialization, and there is no third option available for the traditional sector to survive and remain an independent sector of the economy. In 1874, a British reporter visited Ghana and remarked on the Ghana informal sector that the main street of Accra[4] shows interesting views where people are sitting on small mats on both sides of the street, keeping goods on wooden trays that are offered for sale. He was making the point that informal work existed in Ghana before the precolonial capitalist era, where there existed two types of employment, that is, informal agreement and formal contractual agreement (Thompson, 2009 and Ninsin, 1991). Thus, it gives us a notion that even before the 1970s, there had been an acknowledgment of the "informal sector", even though Keith Hart's seminal work on Ghana and the ILO report on Kenya in the 1970s introduced the "informal sector" as an area of knowledge in the academic world of scholars and provided formal shape to discover and investigate this area of knowledge further.

At the time of the great depression in the 1930s, when formal employment dropped off, informal employment became common and the people who had informal skills became dominant. The failure of the classical economists' movement after the great depression in 1930 gave birth to the emergence of the Keynesian school. The famous economist Milton Keynes and his followers believed full employment could only be achieved by government intervention. In contrast, a paper about Ghana presented at a conference by Keith Hart in 1971, and a study conducted for the economy of Kenya by International Labor Organization (ILO) in 1972, explored that the reality is far away from the mainstream schools of thought, especially in developing economies. They found that a lot of people are employed and working in an informal sector and earning a livelihood although in government statistics and reports they are considered unemployed (Hart, 2012).

4   *Overview of the Shadow Economy*

Since World War II, several forms of government have been practicing with the motto to bring up workers' well-being and reduce income inequalities. Even the International Monetary Fund (IMF), the United Nations (UN), and the World Bank (WB) have been set up to support the neoliberal motto of free market. WB initiated a structural adjustment program especially for low-income countries to promote their economies and boost free movement of money and resources (free market)[5] globally. At that point in time, shadow economy appeared openly, and it was realized and observed not only in low and middle-income countries but also in the most advanced nations of the world (Hart, 2012). So, this public appearance of shadow economy gives us the message that it is not a momentary and residual phenomenon but rather a crucial segment of today's world. Lewis claims in his book *Theory of Economics Growth* that shadow economy will vanish with the economic growth has also been falsified (Schneider and Enste, 2000; Guibourg and Segendorf, 2007; ILO, 2002 and Debrah, 2007).

There was isolation between government control over the economy and the free market from the 1970s till the 2008 economic crisis, but after that the control of government over the free market loosened and the hiding of economic activities from accountability and registration became widespread. The liberal school of thought believed in concoction of power, and they considered money a virtue. This idea has been forwarded by the neoliberal school of thought, which gives way to informalization of economy and decreasing government control over the economy and makes us realize that the free market exists, and government faces challenges to control all the economic activities happening in the country currently (Hart, 2012).

As far as the development of shadow economy is concerned, there are many anxieties about it. The seminal works give positive perception about shadow economy. They consider that with the passage of time, shadow economy will become innovative, proficient, flexible, inventive, elastic, and efficient (Chen et al., 2004). In low-income economies, for some people, shadow economy is an income source; for others it is a source of subsistence; and for some others it adds value to their businesses to grow and develop. As far as the labor market is concerned, shadow economy opens new employments, accommodates extra labor force, and satisfies their necessities of life (Becker, 2004). Just like official economy, the rate of return from shadow economic activities also differs where certain traders and producers earn more as compared to formal counterparts (Williams, 2006 and Lozano, 1989).

International Labor Organization (ILO) accepts that the economic activities that are happening in shadow economy have a huge impact on community and are worthwhile to society, as they are generated by the low-income class of society, even though these activities produce very low income for the participants. Some scholars recognize shadow economy as a hurdle for economic growth and development of an economy. Therefore, they consider that it will disappear as the economies grow, advance, and become industrialized (Chen et al., 2004). So, we can say that since the discovery of shadow economy and the seminal work of Keith Hart (1971, 1973), it is accepted that shadow economy can play an important role

Overview of the Shadow Economy   5

in the economic development of an economy. Shadow economy has a specific market for goods and services where these goods and services are supplied and demanded in the domain of that market; therefore, if there is unemployment in the formal economy, shadow economy can support the official economy by providing jobs to unemployed laborers in order to maintain the development and growth of the overall economy.

To summarize, the pioneer in this area of knowledge, anthropologist and economist Keith Hart, first used the term "informal sector" in 1971. He used the term at the time when he was observing enterprises practice in Ghana's economy. Similarly, the International Labor Organization (ILO), in its report on Kenya in 1972, presented in a more defined way the term "informal sector". Later, this area of knowledge was promoted by Feige (1989),[6] but now Friedrich Schneider[7] dominates the area in terms of scholarly work and research articles, even though it has been discussed before in different contexts, like Furnivall in 1939, Boeke in 1942 and 1961, and Lewis in 1955. Similarly, O'Conner (1983) notified that shadow economy landscapes existed before the industrial revolution in pre-capitalist civilizations. We can also find some sort of informality during the great depression in the 1930s, when unemployment became widespread and informal skilled labor became dominate. In contrast to mainstream schools, that is, Classical and Keynesian, Hart (1973) and ILO (1972) found that there are a lot of people who are working in an informal sector and earning their livelihoods while in government statistics they are considered unemployed. Since World War II, several governments' policies have been put forward with the aim of workers' well-being and a reduction in inequality and poverty. At that point in time shadow economy appeared openly on the surface and was observed not only in low- and middle-income countries but also in the most advanced nations of the world. Lewis, Marx, and the accelerated model considered that informal sector would either be eliminated or would be absorbed by modern industrialization, and there is no third option to remain as an independent sector. But studies like Schneider and Enste (2000), Guibourg and Segendorf (2007), and Portes et al. (1989) discovered that informal sector is not only preserved but also expanded with the passage of time. We can deduce that even before the 1970s, there had been acknowledgment of informal sector, but Keith Hart's seminal work on Ghana and the ILO report on Kenya in the 1970s gave rebirth to this area of knowledge in the academic world and initiated discussion to further discover this area of knowledge.

Taking into consideration the discussion related to OIC member countries where a majority of the OIC member states are developing nations and there is no comprehensive study on shadow economy in OIC countries in terms of discovering its determinants, impact of financial development, and financial inclusion. Therefore, this neglected area needs to be investigated in depth in the context of OIC. This is what the OIC standing committee for economic and commercial cooperation (COMCEC) in its seventh meeting held on February 11, 2016, in Turkey, put forth as its concern about shadow economy and mentioned that "informality" is one of the important issues needed to be addressed in member countries. The economic activities that take place in shadow economy are very

6 Overview of the Shadow Economy

important from the perspective of economic and social policies, especially when it comes to targeting poverty and inequality, because these small and shadow economic activities are conducted by the poor classes of society despite low return. Therefore, these activities further widen the knowledge gap and create additional links to connect the dots.

1.3 Meaning and Definitions of Shadow Economy

Shadow economy is a countable noun, which means economic activities that are complex and complicated for the authorities to know about, as they are unlawful (Longman Dictionary of Contemporary English).

Scholars and economists have provided several names and terms to describe shadow economy, for example, second, black, clandestine, parallel, informal, hidden, underground, unobserved, subterranean, illegal, and so on. Shadow economy is not added in gross domestic product (GDP) or gross national product (GNP) and is also not checked by official authorities and remains outside tax net. In the labor market, it is called grey market. Similarly, other terminologies, like system D, agorism, working in cash, off the books, and under the table are also considered the same terms. In Germany, France, Sweden, Norway and the USA, it is called the Black Market while in other areas it is called hidden economy, illicit work, informal economy, invisible economy, irregular economy/ sector, moonlighting, nonofficial, parallel economy, second economy, subterranean economy, underground economy, unobserved economy, unofficial economy, and unrecorded economy. Even though the nature of shadow economy is latent, each of these terms gives us some idea regarding it. Since its discovery, there has been a considerable part of the economy that is missing from the official accounting, and which provides basis for empirical investigation in economics. All the aforementioned terms demonstrate the reality that shadow economy is a mixture of several economic activities whose investigation is challenging because of its latent nature. The policy makers always tried to combine shadow economy with official economy. Its role is also important in the economy of developing countries because it is a source of income for the poor (Becker et al., 2004; Becker, 2004; The Economist, 2015 and Feige, 2007).

Since its inception, there is no clear agreement on its definition (Öğünç and Yilmaz, 2000), because it is very diversified, heterogeneous, and sophisticated. But we need to provide a basic definition at least to move forward. The basic definition can also help one understand the characteristics and determinants as well as the driving forces of shadow economy.

GDP per capita and productivity of labor force represent the overall income of a country. Yet, it excludes some activities that are not reported in government statistics, that is, household activities, informal activities, and tax evasion money (Smith, 1976 and Bhattacharyya, 1990). Therefore, GDP measurement has a deficiency, as it ignores such activities and underestimates a country's actual and potential national income. Thus, the gap between measured GDP and potential GDP can be called informal sector. Since the discovery of the term "informal sector" by Keith Hart (1971) and ILO (1972) it has been studied by different researchers with different names, for example, shadow economy (Helberger and Knepel, 1988 and Schneider, 2000), informal economy (Castells and Portes, 1989), parallel economy (Del Boca and Forte, 1982), underground economy (Tanzi, 1980 and Tucker, 1982), unobserved economy (Schneider and Enste, 2000), hidden economy (Feige, 1979), and illegal, unregistered and secret economy (Chengelova, 2016).[8]

The activities that are missing from a country's national income (GDP) are normally not subject to rules and regulations. The difference between unregistered economic activities and GDP shape actual or potential economy. This difference and gap gave birth to the notion of "shadow economy", which Cagan expressed by as early as 1958 with the name "irregular economy" and Pissarides and Weber in 1989. But the seminal work of Keith Hart (1971) and ILO (1972) opened this area of knowledge for further study and debate. However, there is still no universal agreement on its definition. Even though numerous economists have defined shadow economy and offered methods for its estimation, there is no agreement on its definition and estimating methodology because of its latent and hidden nature.

Keith Hart (1973) who discovered this area of knowledge and is considered the pioneer of this domain of knowledge defines informal sector, as an economic sector that goes ahead of official service, big companies, and factories. He considers that informal sector activities are beyond government services. According to him, there are two types of informal activities: illegitimate and legitimate activities. By legitimate activities, he means small-scale economic activities that contribute to economic growth, even though at a low level, like homemade production, personal services, and manual labor. On the other hand, by illegitimate activities, he means the activities whose contribution to economic development are doubtful and activities that are not essentially criminal, like pick pocketing, begging, streetwalking, and scavenging.

Part of the World Employment Programme initiative was the International Labor Organization (ILO) report on Kenya in the 1970s, which was led by Hans Singer along with Dharam Gai, Louis Emmerij and Ajit Bhalla (ILO), John Weeks (IDS), as well as Richard Jolly among others. Their work was accepted and assisted by economists and sociologists, and they further said: "One begins to sense that a new school of analysis may be emerging, drawing on work in East and West Africa and using the formal-informal distinction to gain insights into a wide variety of situations." In this report they explain shadow economy as "a way of doing things" described by (i) competitive and unregulated markets, (ii) skill and education gained outside the official schooling system, (iii) easy entrance, (iv) family business ownership, (v) internal means dependency, (vi) tiny operation, (vii) higher labor dependency, and (viii) limited technology (Charmes, 2014).

According to World Bank, informal sector consists of two types. First, it covers that segment of society and economic situation where getting sustenance and livelihood are limited. Second, it captures the avoidance of government regulations by the reasonable businessman.

8   *Overview of the Shadow Economy*

A dominant scholar of this area, Schneider (1986), defines shadow economy as all economic activities that add value to the economy, and that are required to be considered in national income of a country but currently are absent from national accounting. He classified shadow economic activities into nonmarket activities, illegal activities, and legal activities.

By underground economy, Feige (1979: p. 6, 1989) means "those economic activities transactions which unreported or are unmeasured by society's current techniques for observing economic activity". Taking hints from Feige's, the US Labor Department, in 1992, divided shadow economy in these parts: (i) unreported economy, where legal goods are traded but taxes are evaded; (ii) informal economy, in which economic activities take place but are neither regulated nor recognized by the authority, like social security systems, financial credit, and labor contracts violation; (iii) illegal economy, which is based on the selling and buying of prohibited goods and services, for instance, smuggling, corruption, and drugs; and (iv) unrecorded economy, which consists of such concealed revenue-generating economic activities that are not included in GDP, like off-the-book's hiring of workers.

Underground economy is defined by the American Heritage Dictionary of Business Terms as

> business or trade that avoids notice or observation by the government agencies. Illegal activities such as illegal drugs dealings are included in the underground economy. Barter of goods and services that are not reported to government for tax purpose are also a major part of the underground economy.

The black economy is also defined as "those earning of a nation that remains illegally undeclared either as a result of payment in kind or as a means of tax evasion" (Encyclopedia, 2005).

The economic activities that are tacit and concealed from tax authorities come under the shadow economy, while economic activities where dealings take place under a veil from government authorities, remain unrecorded, and take place illegally are considered black or underground economy. The working people in underground economy conceal their income from government officials. Similarly, the businesses in shadow economy are illegal and not regulated by the official authority like drugs, narcotic, smuggling. On the other hand, selling goods on roads and at traffic lights, and gardening jobs fall under grey or informal sector. The type of slavery work where people are forced to work without being paid and payment to the workers in kind and barter transactions are also included in shadow economy.

Shadow economy can also be defined from the perspective of different schools of thought.[9] In the opinion of Dualists, it is an isolated segment that does not have connection with official sector. It is a source income and shelter to the deprived class of society. The emergence and perseverance of shadow economy is due to the failure of industrial progress and economic development to engross all labor force (ILO, 1972). According to Structuralists, it is second to official sector where big industries and firms subordinate small firms and businesses in the informal economy to decrease cost of production and bypass competition (Castells and Portes, 1989). It is the reaction of entrepreneurs and labor to overregulation in the view of Legalists (De Soto, 1989). In these three definitions, one thing is common: shadow economic activities are invisible and not recorded in government accounts (Choi and Thum, 2005). So, it can be said that shadow economy consists of all goods and services that are produced legally or illegally and are kept hidden from the government accounting authority on the following bases: (i) to hide from the minimum legal requirements, like quality of products, safety, wages, and so on, to bypass taxes; (ii) to conceal from administrative and regulatory procedures, that is, fulfilling statistical questionnaires and other forms and requirements; (iii) to escape from paying social security contributions. In all of the these definitions, one thing is common: shadow economic activities are invisible to official record. Thus, to summarize all the above discussions about the definitions of the shadow economy, we can say that the shadow economy is the market value of all unrecorded goods and services produced in a country.

1.4 Measurements of Shadow Economy

In Figure 1.1, we used data from Medina and Schneider (2017). In the figure it is visible that the size of shadow economy in non-OIC countries is 30.57% (of GDP) and in OIC economies it is 34.36% (of GDP). Within the OIC group, the low-income countries have 37.24% of shadow economy size while the high-income countries have 29.17% shadow economy. The size of shadow economy in low-income (LOIC) countries is higher than the high-income (HOIC) countries in OIC countries.

In Figure 1.2 we observe that the size of shadow economy in full sample remains almost at 30%. Similarly, the majority of countries are close to the fitted line, which shows less variation among the nations.

In Figure 1.3, we see that in a subsample of non-OIC countries, the size of shadow economy is around 30%, where the majority of countries are again on the fitted line where the fitted line is significant at 95% level of significance.

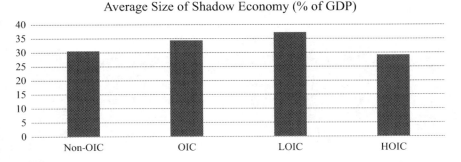

Figure 1.1 Average size of shadow economy (% of GDP) in non-OIC, OIC, LOIC and HOIC

Source: author's own derivation

10 *Overview of the Shadow Economy*

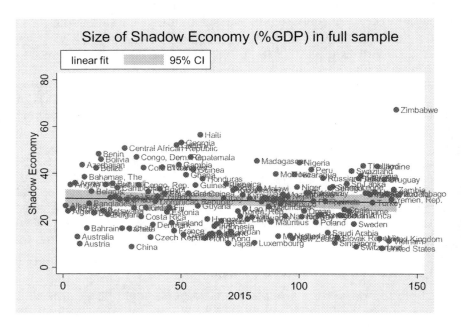

Figure 1.2 Average size of shadow economy (% of GDP) in full sample
Source: author's own derivation

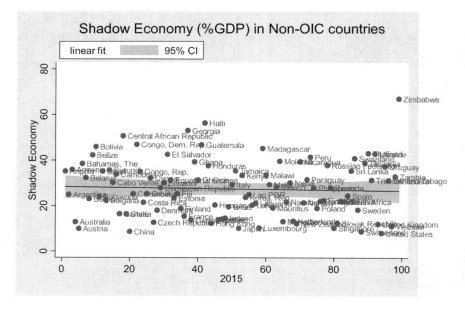

Figure 1.3 Average size of shadow economy (% of GDP) in non-OIC countries
Source: author's own derivation

In Figure 1.4 we witness the average size of shadow economy in case of OIC, that is, the majority of countries cluster above 30% and are on the fitted line where a major part of the fitted line is above 30%, which shows that the size of shadow economy in OIC countries remains higher than non-OIC, which also motivates us to investigate this area in more depth.

Figure 1.5 depicts how the shadow economy completes a circle. If the size of shadow economy is large, the government will receive less revenue due to more tax evasion, causing a government deficit. On the other hand, high government spending and less revenue will create a further deficit, and as a result, fewer funds will be available to spend on public goods and services. Thus, low quality of public goods and services indicates inefficiency of government and consequently more people will join shadow economy.

Compared to non-OIC countries, the large of size of the shadow economy of OIC countries is also depicted by Figure 1.6. Similarly, we also see that the size of shadow economy in the OIC countries is higher than the world average. This large size of shadow economy is one of the sources behind the motivation to carry out this research.

In Figure 1.7, we depicted the size of shadow economy by year for OIC and non-OIC countries. As the figures show, the normal and stationary behavior of shadow economy, which is best fit to predict by the method used in this study, that

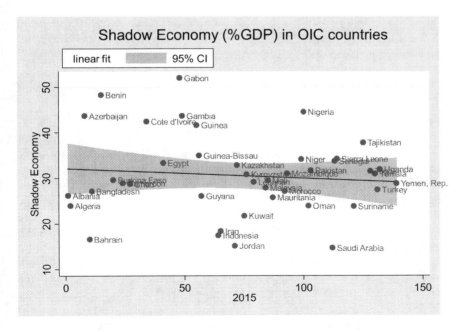

Figure 1.4 Average size of shadow economy (% of GDP) in OIC countries

Source: author's own derivation

12 *Overview of the Shadow Economy*

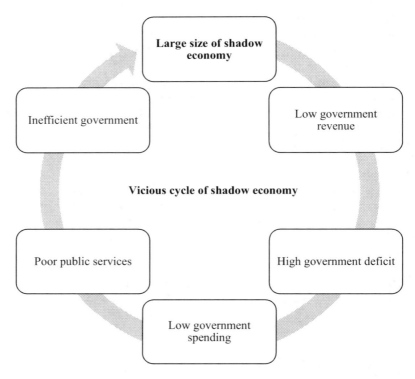

Figure 1.5 Vicious cycle of shadow economy
Source: Alesina (1999)

is, the data is moving around the mean and has small variation. Other methods, such as panel Quantile regression, are needed if there are outliers in the data, but in our case the value is clustered around mean and has less variation, therefore mean-based method is used in this study.

Carter (1984) focused on the partition between informal economy and underground economy by naming the gap "hidden economy". In informal economy, he counted nonmeasurable activities and household sectors, whereas in underground economy he included measurable activities that are irregular and against the law (criminal sector).

According to Smith (1994: p. 4), shadow economy is "market-based production of goods and services, whether legal or illegal, that escapes detection in the official estimates of GDP". Similarly, Bagachwa (1995) divided shadow economy into three types: black market activities (the activities prohibited by the government authorities), informal sectors (small-scale activities), and parallel (illegal by production, though legal by nature). According to Bhattacharyya (1999), production of shadow economy is large because other activities of criminal nature, and

Overview of the Shadow Economy 13

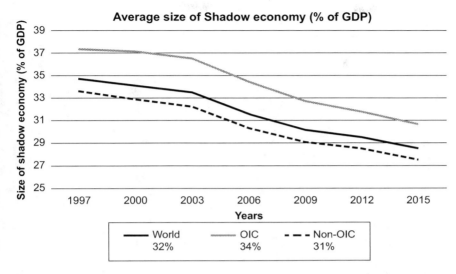

Figure 1.6 Average size of shadow economy (% of GDP) in the World, OIC and non-OIC
Source: author's own derivation

so on, are also part of it. Schneider and Enste (2002) affirmed that each and every economic activity that is not captured in national statistics is also part of shadow economy. They classified these activities into legal, illegal, monetary (market-income economy), and nonmonetary (non-market-income economy) economic activities (see Table 1.1).

There are volunteer economic activities inside the household, which have market values, but are not priced. Therefore, they are not reflected in national income. In shadow economy, most of the activities are small in size, like tiny suppliers, producers, distributors, and craftsmen. According to Schneider and Enste (2002), in shadow economy, the production of goods and services is legal by nature, but illegality comes from the way these goods and services are distributed, or from evasion of taxation. Therefore, the activities of shadow economy give a massage of rejection of regulations, that is, bureaucratic procedures, social security services, labor force rules like maximum working hours and minimum wage. In shadow economy, some activities are by nature illegal, like smuggling, fraud, bribery, drugs, and so on. According to Nikoopour (2005), there are two main divisions of informal economic activities: legality and market transaction, which are discussed in Table 1.2.

From national account perspective, the economic gap (statistical error) between potential GDP and calculated GDP is called shadow economy or nonobserved economy. The goods and services that are produced in the economy are purposely hidden from the government official in order to evade regulations and taxes. The representation of potential economy, shadow economy, and official economy is given in Figure 1.8.

14 *Overview of the Shadow Economy*

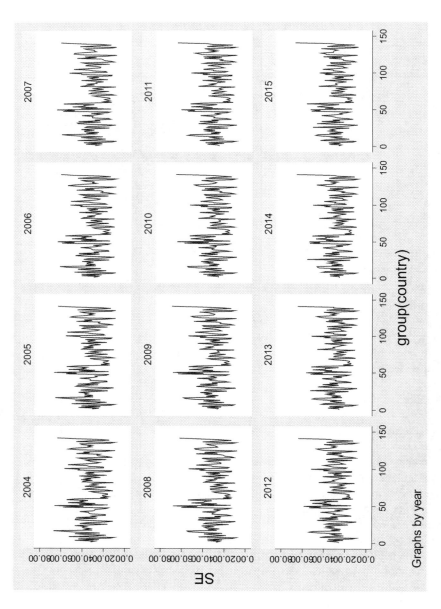

Figure 1.7 Size of shadow economy by years for OIC and non-OIC countries
Source: author's own derivation

Overview of the Shadow Economy   15

Table 1.1 Monetary and nonmonetary activities

Illegal activities

Monetary transactions	*Nonmonetary transactions*
• Trade with stolen goods • Drug dealing and manufacturing • Prostitution • Gambling • Smuggling • Fraud • Etc.	• Barter of drugs • Barter of stolen goods • Barter of smuggled goods, etc. • Producing or growing drugs for own use • Theft goods for own use

Legal activities

Monetary transactions		*Nonmonetary transactions*	
Tax evasion	*Tax avoidance*	*Tax evasion*	*Tax avoidance*
• Unreported income from self-employment • Wages, salaries, and assets from unreported work related to legal services and goods	• Employee discounts, fringe benefits	• Barter of legal goods and services	• All do-it yourself work and neighbor help

Source: Schneider and Hametner (2014)

Table 1.2 Sectors of shadow economy by legality and market transaction

Sectors	*Market transactions*	*Production nature*	*Distribution nature*
Informal	Practiced	Legal	Legal
Illegal	Practiced	Illegal	Illegal
Household	Not practiced	Legal	Legal
Hidden	Practiced	Legal	Legal

Adopted from Hussmanns (2004)

Dell'Anno (2007) classifies shadow economic activities into three main categories: illegal, underground/hidden/irregular, and informal/unmeasured. The illegal economy consists of totally prohibited activities by the government officials. It contains illegal and even criminal activities, for example, smuggling, drug dealing, gang activity, and so on. The production and distribution both are not permissible of such kinds of goods and services. Next is the unmeasured, or informal, economy, which is unmeasured and remains outside GDP calculation. This includes street vendors, agricultural output by smallholders, beggars, unpaid home workers and small producers, and so on. The production and distribution of these activities are legal. Subsequently, the economic activities that

16 *Overview of the Shadow Economy*

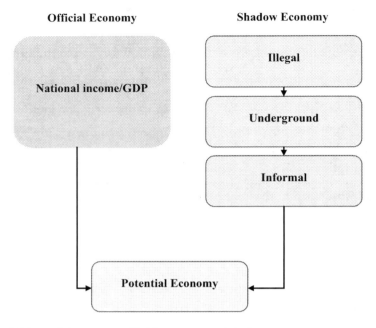

Figure 1.8 Potential economy, official economy, and shadow economy
Source: author's own derivation

are intentionally concealed from government authority and are not declared to be taxed are called irregular or hidden or underground economy, such as industries, firms, companies, restaurants, and so on, who hide or under-declare their income to evade taxes. The production of these activities is legal, but distribution is not. The distribution is given in Figure 1.9.

Many researchers have tried to find the reasons for shadow economy and have seen its impact on formal economy. Their findings vary from country to country based on the methodologies they used. Yet, a common finding among all studies is that shadow economy is growing, and it is 10% to 25% of the formal economy in developing countries. Schneider (2002) studied shadow economy of 21 OECD[10] countries and 22 transaction countries and found that shadow economy is 15% to 30% of the official economy of OECD and transaction economies respectively. Overregulation and tax burden are the main causes for shadow economy. In another study, Schneider (2005) finds that transition economies, including South America and Africa, have bigger shadow economy as compared to OECD economies. By investigating the economies of Czech Republic and Slovakia, Orviská et al. (2006) conclude that shadow economy as a percentage of official economy is 21.8% and 23.2% respectively. Karlinger (2009) studies transaction, developing, and OECD economies and finds that labor market regulation and taxes are

Overview of the Shadow Economy 17

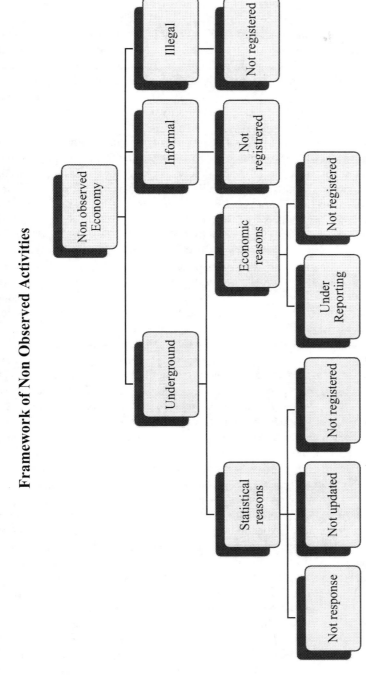

Figure 1.9 Distribution of shadow economy
Source: Dell'Anno (2007)

18 Overview of the Shadow Economy

the main contributing factors for shadow economy. On the other hand, exploring determinants of shadow economy in 69 countries, Friedman et al. (2000) depict that it is the excessive regulation and corruption that promptly influence shadow economy, while high marginal tax rates have little impact on it. By applying MIMIC model (Multiple Indicator, Multiple Cause Model) and using data from 1990 to 2005 for 21 OECD economies, Feld and Schneider (2010) identify that excessive regulation, unemployment, and taxes impact shadow economy directly, and such influence is bigger in developing countries as compared to transition economies. On the other hand, individual morality and institutions quality have a negative impact on shadow economy.

It is well-known that most of the OIC economies are developing and one of the important issues with developing economies regarding formulating economic policies is the nonexistence of efficient, timely, accurate, reliable, and consistent data. Even though national statistics are available and in line with the national account system, still these statistics deteriorate in terms of inaccuracy and deficiency of valuating economic variables. Similarly, in these countries, data collection is problematic and estimation methods suffer from deficiency. In the same way, firms and businesses keep information secret from government authorities. Authenticity and accuracy of economic statistics and data are important to implement and formulate efficient and effective economic policies and allocate resources in the best possible way. By investigating the size of shadow economy in OIC economies, more comprehensive data and statistics will be provided, which will lead to more efficient and effective economic policies.

From a fiscal policy perspective, shadow economy reduces tax revenue and results in higher and more costly public expenditure. In order to manage taxes and expenditure, it is important to know the magnitude, frequency, and size of shadow economy to overcome such problems. Keeping in mind all these issues, the measurement of shadow economy becomes an important concern for policy makers. If the size of shadow economy is large, it creates governance problems, signaling the presence of excessive regulations, and understates national income and other macroeconomic variables. If macroeconomic variables present wrong information, then the policies based on such variables will also be incorrect and inefficient (Schneider and Enste, 2000, 2002 and Eilat and Zinnes, 2002).

The economists and policy makers are interested in shadow economy because shadow economy creates issues of budget deficit and reduction in tax revenue, which in turn reduces government expenditure on public services like health care, human capital development, infrastructure, and so on (Johnson et al., 2000). According to Fuest and Riedel (2009), bigger tax evasion in an economy is a sign of the existence of large shadow economy. Similarly, it causes reduction in tax revenue, which as a result even threatens accurate functioning of the government (Franzoni, 1998).

Shadow economy exists in all types of economies in different shapes and in unlikely places. Many researchers and economists have studied shadow economy from different perspectives by using different methodologies, and have got different results because of the complex, dynamic, and heterogenous nature of present-day economies (Becker, 2004 and Schneider, 2005) as well as the different characteristics, nature, determinants and sizes of shadow economies in different countries.

For their livelihoods, people engage in different economic activities, generally at the micro level. With the passage of time and with economic development, the order and supervision of these activities gave birth to the rules and regulations of the markets. At the beginning, countries did not succeed in implementing market regulations, although they tried their best to order and formulize it. Economists have found both in advanced and developing countries that people constantly try to hide their incomes from government regulations and persistently alter economic activities to avoid rulings. If shadow economic activities go beyond regulations, and if informal economy is unregulated, then we can say that before regulation of the markets there were unregulated markets, which are as old as official economy (Malek and Arshad, 2017).

At the start of economics education, only official economic activities were studied, and informal sector was ignored until the discovery of the term "informal sector" by Keith Hart in 1971 and ILO in 1973. In order to capture overall activities from the 1990s and onward, scholars started using the term "informal economy" in place of "informal sector" (Becker, 2004; Hart, 1971 and ILO, 1972). We conclude our discussion with the definition provided by Frey and Schneider (2000): "national income generated by those non-reporting productive or value-added activities that is supposedly to be calculated in the Gross National Product (GNP)" and according to Bovi and Dell'Anno (2010: p. 20): "the value-added activities that the official statistics do not register although they should".

1.5 Economic Impacts of Shadow Economy

The goods and services produced in shadow economy are invisible to government officials and are not included in macroeconomic variables. Therefore, the variables misrepresent the picture of whole economy because goods and services that are produced in shadow economy are not recorded and consequently leads to misleading economic policies. This is the reason the discussion on shadow economy started in the mid-twentieth century, which helped to consider this ignored and neglected sector of the economy and to have accuracy in the governments' official statistics. Similarly, it was considered a crucial social and economic issue. In the third half of twentieth century, it turned into a universal issue, which also gave birth to its investigation in academic circles (Erdinç, 2012).

The most convincing effect of shadow economy is on the development of economic policies. Because of the large size of shadow economy, the macroeconomic fundamentals turn out to be defective and unreliable; consequently, the policies using these indicators as a basis also become misguided and futile. The firms and businesses that operate in shadow economy also have advantages over official firms in terms of having cheap labor and other factors of production and therefore can produce the same goods with low cost compared to official firms. Therefore, these firms have comparative advantages over official firms and thus create unfair competition in the official market. The goods and services

20   *Overview of the Shadow Economy*

produced in shadow economy can command the price they want because of there are no legal rules and regulations. Therefore, firms can disturb the market forces by selling goods below the market price because they have a comparatively low cost, and thus hurt the official firms. Shadow economy also creates anxiety in the social security system because the nonpayment of taxes reduces government revenue. On the other hand, honest citizens lose their trust in government because they face an additional burden of tax increases due to decreases in government revenue and budget deficits.

In general, shadow economy negatively affects the whole economy, subverts the social and economic structure of the overall economy, and undermines macroeconomic fundamentals (Erdinç, 2012). According to Saraç and Başar (2014), shadow economy over-reports unemployment rates, as the people who are engaged in shadow economy are also recorded as unemployed in official statistics, even though they are earning from shadow economy. In the same way, even though the prices of goods and services are low in shadow economy, because of absence from government statistics, the general price level is over-reported. The distribution of welfare is also devastating, because shadow economy leads to an unjust distribution of economic resources. Conversely, shadow economy provides training for fresh and unskilled laborers to develop their skills and get experience from informal sector and then utilized their expertise in official sector. Similarly, because of the low cost of production, the goods and services that are produced in informal sector are cheaper and inferior and come under the income range of the poorer classes of society.

Furthermore, the additional labor force that the official economy fails to absorb is getting employed in shadow economy, while at the time of economic crises and recession, shadow economy plays a role as a safety net and safeguard. So, the role of shadow economy is like a "social relief valve" at the time of economic hurdle through generating jobs and revenue breaks and adding to additional sources of production (Becker, 2004 and Arias and Khamis, 2008). Moreover, one of the additional reasons people like shadow economy is that it offers flexible labor hours and terms and conditions (Carter, 1984). According to Saraç and Başar (2014), shadow economy is a source of capital accumulation and plays an important role in economic growth, because 66% of the income generated in shadow economy is spent in formal economy, which helps in boosting aggregate demand and the resulting economic prosperity. In the UK, in the long run, shadow economy boosts aggregate consumption expenditure (Bhattacharyya, 1993).

In response to a question, Milton Friedman (1947) explained the economic reason for black bazaar or informal sector and held a position that

> The black market was a way of getting around government controls. It was a way of enabling the free market to work. It was a way of opening up, enabling people. You want to trade with me, and the law won't let you. But that trade will be mutually beneficial to both of us.

He further clarifies black market in the context of free market where two parties agree to trade with each other because of their mutual benefits, but the law does not allow them to have mutual benefits.

Overview of the Shadow Economy 21

Introducing government directives to the market creates an exchange of goods and services between two parties where one party benefits at the expense of other party. Therefore, in order to obtain joint benefits, they enter into a voluntary contract in a black market so as to evade government regulations. Friedman remarks that the breach of rules is an objectionable feature of the black market but following all rules and regulations of government regardless of good law and bad law is not ethically good because there comes a stage where "there is a higher law than the legislative law" (Friedman, 1947).[11] This passage from Milton Friedman gives us a message that every law of government is not to be obeyed, especially when it creates hurdles for the free exchange of goods and services and brings benefits to one party at the cost of other. This is why the black market comes into existence where goods and services are freely traded and where entering into a contract brings mutual benefits to both parties. It looks like that he is more inclined toward the Legalist school of shadow economy, which considers shadow economy as a response to overregulation of government.

Notes

1 This economy consisted of fishing, agriculture, livestock, and small trading. But keep in mind that in the modern day, the agriculture sector has engaged major portion of the labor force in most of the developing nations, but before colonization, almost 80% of the workforce was involved in agriculture sector.
2 Capitalist production means the method of production of commodity that was used by capitalists owing to the resources of production and taking advantage of worker wages to receive surplus value.
3 Commodity production means the production for exchange in the market. At the initial stage of goods exchange, there was a barter system whereby people exchanged one good for another. With the passage of time, goods exchange was replaced with special commodity, that is, money that was detached from other goods instinctively.
4 It is the capital of Ghana.
5 It is a market structure where market force, that is, demand, and supply determine the prices of goods and services that are free from state interference, monopolists etc.
6 Edgar L. Feige is an emeritus professor of economics at the University of Wisconsin – Madison. In his famous book titled *The Underground Economies: Tax Evasion and Information Distortion* (Cambridge University Press, 1989), he discusses shadow economy in detail.
7 Friedrich Schneider is Professor of Economics at Johannes Kepler University of Linz, Austria, and a research professor at the DIW Berlin, Germany. He has published extensively on shadow economy in leading journals, including *The American Economic Review*, *The Quarterly Journal of Economics*, *The Economic Journal*, and the *Journal of Economic Literature*. He has also published numerous book chapters and books but his famous book is The Shadow Economy, with Dominik H. Enste (Cambridge University Press, 2002).
8 In this study, we use the term "shadow economy" alternative to informal economy, unofficially economy, unrecorded economy, unobserved economy and unregistered economy.
9 The school of thoughts will be discussed in detail in Chapter 5.
10 Organisation for Economic Co-operation and Development
11 Public Broadcasting Service (PBS). (2000, January 10). Interview with Milton Friedman. Available at www.pbs.org/wgbh/commandingheights/shared/minitext/int_mil tonfriedman.html#2.

2 Shadow Economy and Islamic Finance

Even though shadow economy is an old phenomenon, an interest in investigating it has emerged in the last two decades. Researchers have investigated it from multiple perspectives, such as estimation of its size, causes, and impact on society, but the stance of Islamic finance on shadow economy is hardly investigated. Therefore, this chapter is dedicated to discussing shadow economy from an Islamic finance perspective. Thus, it covers the Islamic economic system and shadow economy, objectives of Shariah and shadow economy, shadow economy, multiplier and crowding out effects in Islamic economy, brief history of Islamic finance, informal finance and OIC countries, Islamic banking sector and shadow economy, role of Islamic micro financial institutions and the shadow economy, and the way forward for inclusive micro takaful.

2.1 Islamic Economic System and Shadow Economy

The Islamic economic system is in favor of a free market but subject to Islamic values in the fields of consumption, exchange, production, and distribution. The Islamic economic system is flexible in terms of private ownership and social justice to ensure balance, equality, happiness, and reciprocity in obligation. Two more concepts related to Islamic economy are objectivism and moralism. Islamic economic system believes in objectivism. In other words, an Islamic economy is realistic and comprehensive in approach (on the one hand, it accepts the reality of existence of informal system and therefore provides regulations for it, while on the other hand it approaches informal sector along with formal sector). Furthermore, it also has a place for moralism. For example, in an Islamic economic system, the market is free, thus the demand and supply forces are free to push prices upward and downward according to the market condition. But this free movement of market is subject to Islamic moral values, which means that the market should not be driven by monopoly and the market forces should not be disrupted (Anwar, 1987 and Sadr, 1982).

2.2 Objectives of Shariah vis-à-vis Shadow Economy

There are three main features of an Islamic economic system. First, it ensures the certainty of basic needs and sustenance of livelihood. Second, it promotes

DOI: 10.4324/9781003329954-2

equal distribution of resources, and, finally, it eliminates distortion in the market via eradication of extreme inequalities, monopoly, speculation, and so on. Similarly, one of the main objectives of Shariah is to protect life while providing basic needs, which is the responsibility of the Islamic state (Kamali, 2005). Therefore, the informal sector can be studied from the objective of Shariah perspective in two scenarios. First, taking care of the people who are deprived and remain a part of informal sector, which falls under the objective of protection of life. Second, the Shariah aims to control all kinds of illegal activities, for example, trade with stolen goods, drug dealing and manufacturing, prostitution, gambling, smuggling, fraud, and so on, which are taking place in informal economy. This latter aspect comes under the objective of protection of wealth.

2.3 Shadow Economy, Multiplier and Crowding Out Effects in Islamic Economy

It is interesting to study the multiplier and crowding out effects from an Islamic economic perspective and analyze their effects on the shadow economy. In order to finance fiscal deficit, a government will borrow from the market, and as a result, market interest rate will increase. This increase will create problems for private businesses, especially small- and medium-scale businesses, and the result will be shrinking of their businesses because of the high financing rate. So, the next option available to them is to join the informal sector and look for cheaper sources of funds. On the other hand, in case of an Islamic economic system, if there is any budget deficit, the government will request financial institutions to provide funds based on *qard hasan*, *zakat*, *sadaqat*, and so on. By using these Islamic instruments, governments can overcome the problem of shortage of funds without hurting general capital market (Kabbara, 2014 and Yusoff, 2006). In this case, there will be no crowding out effect, and, as a result, businesses will stay in official sector of the economy and will not be pushed toward shadow economy.

Another interesting aspect of the Islamic economic system is that it consists of different kinds of Islamic products like *zakat*, *sadaqat*, and other types of charity products. All these funds are obtained from the savings of rich people and make a part of the consumption of poor people. When such portions of savings are channeled toward consumption, marginal propensity to consume (MPC) will increase, while multiplier will decrease. A reduced multiplier will not open the doors to an increase in demand for financing. Consequently, the rate of financing will remain the same and there will be no crowding out effect. On the other hand, this situation will deter individuals from joining the shadow economy, because of an increase in disposable income of the deprived class of society. As a result, people will stay and operate in official economy and will begin their businesses in the formal economy. If the *zakat* and *sadaqat* and other charitable funds are distributed through financial institutions, it will increase financial inclusion and reduce financial exclusion (Mohieldin et al., 2011).

2.4 Brief History of Islamic Finance

The discussion on Islamic economic and interest free system began from the mid-twentieth century. Islamic countries participated in international trade and international financial transition through banks, but the main challenge faced at the time was that the banking system was conventional and interest-based. Therefore, there was a need for a financial system that would be free from interest and Shariah repugnant products, and compatible with Shariah principles. Therefore, in the late 1960s and 1970s, governments and national financial institutions of some Muslims countries arranged high-level conferences where the concept and theory of Islamic finance was discussed.

Thus, the first Islamic bank was established in 1975 in Dubai with the intention to have a financial system that was not only in line with Shariah principles but also contributed to the betterment of society. In terms of market capitalization and assets growth, it boasts a presence in over 70 countries today, including non-Muslims jurisdictions. Maintaining an excellent growth rate and having good market capitalization, currently its assets are over 2.2 trillion dollars and are expected to grow by 9.4%, reaching 3.8 trillion dollars, in 2022. As new Islamic financial institutions are established, it is expected that the upward trend in growth will continue in coming years (Reuters and Standard, 2016). Islamic finance is pushed forward by OIC countries looking to the potential of Muslim populations. It is a way forward to boost financial inclusion from both formal and informal sectors. Behind such significant growth and development, one of the main strengths of Islamic finance is the acceptance of sustainable development goals (SDGs). Additionally, Islamic finance promotes small- and medium-sized enterprises (SMEs), micro-takaful, and Islamic social business (ISB). Besides all other advantages of Islamic finance, the aforementioned products are highly significant, because in a majority of the OIC economies more than 50% of economic activities are made by small businesses, and the informal sector is 34% of GDP. Therefore, these products are hitting the root of poverty, because they are not only catering to the formal sector but at the same time targeting the informal sector as well.[1]

2.5 Informal Finance and OIC Countries

Traditionally, there are two expected reasons for the informal financial sector to grow and develop. First, there are some groups of people who refuse to become part of the current financial sector. Second, some people remain away from the official sector because of the failure of formal finance to accommodate some kinds of transactions. In the context of OIC economies, one of the main reasons for people to stay away and remain excluded from the current financial sector is that the entire financial system is not in line with their religious beliefs. This is because the conventional financial system is based on interest and other Shariah-impermissible activities like excessive speculation, *gharar*, gambling, and so on (Mushtaq, 2017). Consequently, people have to find their own ways of savings, credit, loans, and so on. Therefore, Islamic finance can play an important role in bringing in these excluded people to the formal financial market. Another reason for the refusal of the current financial system is a severe lack of trust. On the one hand, many banks and financial institutions become bankrupt, while on the other hand there is fear among the masses that these financial institutions will break down or, due to political instability, the government will seize their money and freeze their bank accounts. After implementation of the Islamic financial system, the money that is absent from the formal financial system can be brought into the system because there is a lot of wealth in the informal market, which is going out to other nations or is hoarded in other forms.

If the Islamic financial system is expanded and pushed up by the government, most of this money will be brought in to the formal system through Islamic finance. Modern fintech and outstanding financial facilities services, along with competitive investment returns, are also crucial for the development of the Islamic financial system. Similarly, there is also a need to develop the confidence of people with regard to Islamic finance. Usually, conventional financial institutions take deposits from the common people and then provide these to wealthy people (only to those who have collateral), but they exclude the deprived, poor, and remote part of society. The people who are excluded from the formal financial system due to strict collateral requirements in conventional financing (Siddiqi, 2006) can be brought into the official sector with the help of Islamic finance. This gap can be filled by Islamic Financial Institutions (IFIs) by using Islamic products like *qard hassan*, micro financing, micro-takaful, Islamic social business models, and so on. Bringing this part of the society to the formal sector on the one hand will bring additional revenue to the government, and on the other hand, the economic conditions will become better, which will result in the welfare of the overall economy. This is what the UN's Sustainable Development Goals and objectives of Shariah try to achieve.

Informal finance is not observable and therefore it is not part of the official statistics. There are some deposits, savings, loans, and black money markets in informal sector. According to World Bank, there are some credits and savings associations that consist of small groups of people in which a leader will collect the amount from all members periodically. The first payment will be received by the leader because of management of the fund and the others will get the payment on a rotation basis through a lottery draw system.

There are two propositions regarding the informal financial market. One group of scholars favors it while the other is against. The scholars who favor the informal financial market argue that it represents the true picture of the economy. They consider an imbalanced structure of the economy, like overregulation, to be the main culprit behind reducing the incentive to operate in a formal economy as the cause of its development (Chen et al., 2004 and Becker, 2004). The second, and decidedly main, factor is artificially low interest rates, which discourage saving. Another contributing factor is the allocation of credit to specific regions, sectors, or groups at the expense of others. These scholars base their arguments from specific cases from the OIC member countries, for example, Yemen, where the

26 *Shadow Economy and Islamic Finance*

informal banking sector was considered a source of economic stability for a long period of time. On the other hand, opponents see many problems with the informal market. They consider it inherently restricted, small-scale, and limited to a small part of the population. Its fast growth is open to abuse, fraud, and deception. It is costly not only for the government but also for the common people. This is because when taxes, fees, and other payments are evaded by people in the informal sector, government loses its revenue, which as a result shrinks government's developmental expenditure (Dell'Anno et al., 2007; Dell'Anno, 2003; Ott, 2002 and Frey and Weck-Hanneman, 1984).

2.6 Islamic Banking Sector and Shadow Economy

There is no comprehensive study available on the subject, but according to the survey conducted on the performance of Islamic banking in terms of informal financial sector, financial inclusion is not convincing. The study was conducted in Egypt by Elias Kazarian and his findings are interesting. First, he found that the upsurge in Islamic banking deposits mainly took place because people tend to transfer their money from conventional banks to Islamic banks. In other words, financially excluded people have not really been brought into the financial system. Instead, it is only a conversion of deposits from conventional banks to Islamic banks. Therefore, the growth in Islamic finance does not mean that new and financially excluded people have been brought into the official financial system. Second, Islamic banking's focus is only on big metropolises, and little or no consideration is given to rural areas. It means that these banks are just like conventional banks and their motive is to focus on the wealthy and rich sectors of society as compared to the poor and neglected parts. Finally, just like conventional banks, Islamic bank customers are also wealthy, that is, they have collateral and there is no space for poor and lower income segments of society (Warde, 2000).

2.7 Role of Islamic Micro Financial Institutions (IMFI) in Shadow Economy

In the late 1970s, Islamic cooperative insurance was introduced with the name of takaful in Egypt and Sudan. As compared to conventional insurance, which is based on interest, takaful is based on the Islamic principles of mutual cooperation and protection (*ta'awun*). The growth rate of takaful is tremendous with a market capitalization of US$14.9 billion in 2015 and it is expected to grow fast in the future.

Going one step further and taking into consideration the Islamic rules of mutual cooperation, in 1997, another model of takaful evolved in Lebanon, where the first Islamic micro-takaful was established with the aim of not only mutual cooperation but at the same time special consideration was given to target the poor and neglected class of the economy (ICMIF takaful, 2010). Micro-takaful is defined as "pre-emptive efforts at providing insurance services to low income or marginalized groups in a manner where they participate in the design, development, management and governance of such product, services or institutions" (ICMIF, 2015). After that, it grew rapidly and spread among other Muslim countries like Pakistan, Malaysia, Indonesia, and Bahrain. The focus was not solely given to the formal sector of the economy; rather they adopted a comprehensive approach by covering both the official economy and shadow economy. The benefit of this product is that it is inclusive by nature, which includes both formal and informal businesses under one broad umbrella, and at the same time it is considered one of the most hopeful and optimistic products among all other Shariah-based financial products.

There are reasons behind the great expectations from micro-takaful as it directly targets an abandoned part of the society. Another positive aspect of micro-takaful is that it reduces financial exclusion by including businesses and workers from the informal sector into the formal. It is the concern of every government to make enterprises and entrepreneurs a part of the official economy. The convergence of micro-takaful can be increased by adding people from the informal sector, which will open the doors to introducing additional financial products and will reduce the cost of administration, marketing, and distribution. The model of micro-takaful is based on mutual cooperation, therefore this model of partner-agent reduces pooling risk between formal and informal sectors. It supports the neglected part of the society in terms of providing security, harmony, signs of attachment, efforts for joint benefits and mutual advantages, as well as maintaining their financial needs. Micro-takaful can be supported by a *zakat* fund where the coverage can be extended to all segments of the informal society. Similarly, the model of *waqf* can be used to support the poor class of society and make them financially stable, which is not only in line with Sustainable Development Goals (SDGs) of the United Nations but also in line with Maqasid al-Shariah (Mohieldin et al., 2011).

2.8 The Way Forward for Inclusive Micro-Takaful

Micro-takaful plays an important role in the improvement of the living standards of the underprivileged class of society in terms of creating an environment of mutual benefits among them. It is a source of financial inclusion of the people who are excluded from the official sector. It is an essential tool for eradication of poverty and developing resilience in societies against natural calamities. Just as takaful is used to secure the main stream or official sector of the economy, micro-takaful is much broader, which includes both sectors of the economy, that is, formal and informal (which has traditionally been outside of the scope of the conventional insurance framework).

To summarize, the Islamic finance model is unique and comprehensive and seeking the overall welfare of both formal and informal segments. Islamic finance is driven by norms, ethics, and values of Islamic principles where priority is given to promote economic and social justice by providing support to the deprived segments of the society and channeling the benefits of financial resources and facilities to both sectors. In Islamic finance, there is no concept of survival of the fittest in relation to a conventional financial system, which favors the fittest (customer with collateral).

28 *Shadow Economy and Islamic Finance*

2.9 Conclusion

To summarize, in this chapter we have observed that shadow economy is sophisticated and there are not only controversies regarding its different methods of measurement but also in its definition. Historically speaking, it has been observed since in the middle of twentieth century, even though some write-ups are also found in the mid-twentieth century, but it has been discovered and properly recognized in the world of academia by Keith Hart (1971) and ILO (1972). It is well-known that most of the OIC economies are developing and one of the important issues in developing economies regarding formulating economic policies is the nonexistence of efficient, timely, accurate, reliable, and consistent data on one hand while on the other hand there is a huge portion of shadow economy, that is, 34.36% in OIC states that is not recognized in national statistics. Even though national statistics are available and in line with the national account system, still it deteriorates in terms of inaccuracy and deficiency of valuation of economic variables and economic activities. Similarly, in these countries, data collection is problematic and estimation methods suffer from deficiency. In these countries, firms and businesses keep information secret from government authorizes because of involvement in illicit and shadow activities. Authenticity and accuracy of economic statistics and data are important to implement and formulate efficient and effective economic policies and allocate resources in a proper way. So, if the size of shadow economy is large, it creates governance problems, signaling the presence of excessive regulations, understates national income and other macroeconomic variables. If macroeconomic variables present wrong information, then the policies based on such variables will also be incorrect and inefficient.

It can also be concluded that shadow economy exists in all types of economies in different shapes and in unlikely places. Many researchers and economists have studied shadow economy from a different perspective by using different methodologies and achieving distinct objectives because of the complex, dynamic, and heterogeneity of present-day economies (Becker, 2004 and Schneider, 2005). However, characteristics, nature, determinants, and size of shadow economy differ from country to country. Researchers have studied shadow economy in advanced and transaction countries, while less concentration has been given to developing countries. It is also realized that there is a knowledge gap regarding shadow economy in the context of OIC countries. Furthermore, the chapter also put forward the seriousness of the large size of shadow economy.

Note

1 IFC (International Finance Corporation). 2014. *Islamic Banking Opportunities Across Small and Medium Enterprises in MENA*. World Bank, Washington DC.

3 Main Causal Factors of Shadow Economy

As we discussed in Chapter 1, it is very difficult to define shadow economy because of its very diversified, heterogeneous, and sophisticated nature. Just like the definition, it is also important to understand the main causes of informal economy. Therefore, this chapter is dedicated to discussing the main causal factors of shadow economy, which include tax and social security contributions, intensity of regulations, public sector service, official economy, and unemployment.

3.1 Tax and Social Security Contribution

Tax burden and social security contribution are the main causes of shadow economy; economists are always concerned about tax burden as it has a huge impact on time distribution between labor and leisure (Schneider, 1994a, 1994b, 1997, 1998a, 2000, 2003, 2005; Tanzi, 1999; Giles, 1999a; Mummert and Schneider, 2002; Giles and Tedds, 2002 and Dell'Anno, 2003). The expansion and size of shadow economy will be large, as the gap between after-tax revenue and cost of labor in formal economy is high. Because of huge income from informal activities and investment opportunities in human and real capital, tax reforms are only capable of soothing shadow economy but cannot reduce it considerably (Schneider, 2005).

Many empirical studies found that taxation has a significant impact on shadow economy. In advanced countries like Austria, direct tax, intensity of regulations, and complication in the tax system have significant impacts of shadow economy. The same is correct for Denmark, Sweden, Norway, and Germany (Klovland, 1984; Kirchgaessner, 1983 and Schneider, 1986).

According to neoclassical economists, increase in marginal tax rate has a positive impact on labor-leisure decisions and where substitution effect will overcome income effect and workers will shift to shadow economy, which as a result leads to welfare loss and reduce efficiency. Such loss will be recovered if the welfare of people who are working in shadow economy are taken into consideration (Thomas, 1992). Cebula (1997) found for the economy of the United States that a 1% increase in marginal federal personal income tax rate will lead to a raise in shadow economy by 1.4%. Hill and Kabir (1996) empirically found that replacing direct tax with indirect tax is not fruitful while marginal tax rate is better

DOI: 10.4324/9781003329954-3

30   *Main Causal Factors of Shadow Economy*

than average tax rates. Another study was conducted by Johnson et al. (1998b), who observed direct association between corporate tax burden and size of shadow economy. They also found that it is not higher tax rates but ineffectiveness and implementation of the tax system as well as government regulations that raises the size of shadow economy. Similarly, corruption and bribery amount, political and bureaucratic systems, and administrative efficiency significantly impact taxpayers and the relationship of the government with the public.

According to Marinov (2008), people are joining shadow economy because they are not happy with the government due to insufficiency in organisational ability and lack of public services. A study conducted by Friedman et al. (2000) and Ott (1998) found a positive relationship of corruption and unproductive spending of government with shadow economy, as it leads to additional burden on tax payers.

In addition, an interesting finding from Torgler et al. (2010) reveals that education expenditure is positively correlated with shadow economy. Similarly, welfare beneficiaries and social welfare systems are discouraging people to work in formal economy. Because these jobless people are receiving money from the welfare system, they would not be willing to work in official economy in order to benefit from both, that is, shadow economy and welfare system (Schneider, 2008).

A study done by Gulzar et el. (2010) for the economy of Pakistan found that the size of shadow economy is positively affected by tax evasion, which as a result leads to slowing down development of official economy and creates poverty and inequality. The structure of the economy and value added tax (VAT) provide a way to implement taxes in official economy merely and escort shadow economy at the cost of official economy because of diverting economic means from official economy to shadow economy. Consequently, tax evasion will increase and will create hurdles to increasing taxes even at a time of economic growth and development.

According to Schneider (2005) and Giles and Johnson (2000), the size of informal economy rises with an increase in tax burden and there is a universal agreement that it is the tax burden that pushes people to the shadow economy, because they search for different means to earn their livelihoods and therefore participate in shadow economy. The decision of people to join informal sector creates an additional hurdle for the government officials to raise and reform the tax system. Similarly, more people will participate in shadow economy if the after-tax earnings and cost of labor difference is large, because less-disposable income remains with people for spending and saving, therefore, encouraging people to partake in shadow economy. For this reason, the higher the difference between after-tax revenue and cost of labor, the more the incentive to go for informal economy (Schneider and Enste, 2000). Therefore, in order to reduce the size of shadow economy, it is necessary to reform the tax system and social security contribution system. Joo (2011) and Spiro (1993) investigate that the decrease in tax rate is not a convincing policy against shadow economy. Reduction in tax rate will only smooth the way for shadow economy rather than reduce it.

Main Causal Factors of Shadow Economy 31

There are many reasons that compel individuals not to leave shadow economy, like social and personal connection, maximum earning from informal sector as compared to formal economy. Even though a huge decrease in direct tax is not a good policy to reduce the size of the shadow economy in the case of Austria (Schneider, 1994b and Schneider and Enste, 2000). The same study of Joo (2011) for the economy of Korea explores that easiness in rules and regulations to join official economy is a better solution to shrink shadow economy as compared to a decrease in tax rates. He further discusses that easiness in entry to formal economy will reduce income inequality, while reduction in tax rates even though it reduces shadow economy would at the same time boost income inequality. Similarly, the size of shadow economy reduces along with both easiness in rules to enter an official economy as well as reduction in tax rates. This study contradicts others who find a significant impact of taxes on the hours spent in the shadow economy, revenue from the official economy, and the size of shadow economy (Schneider, 1994a; Johnson et al., 1998a and Schneider and Enste, 2000).

Sookram and Watson (2008) explore that it is the fear of detection by the regulators that has an impact on the decision to choose shadow economy or not. If someone feels they are about to be detected by the tax authority, the person will not participate in shadow economy; otherwise participation would be sure. Likewise, a change in tax rates is negligible in terms of deciding to participate in shadow economy or not.

The cost of labor rises, and real wages decrease with an increase in social security contribution. Social security contribution is an additional burden on producers, too, as it increases cost of production and reduces revenue, but if such cost of production is transferred to the workers by reducing their wages, then the workers will join shadow economy in order to cover the wages that have been reduced by social security contributions. Similarly, in order to reduce production cost, producers will also look for factors of production from shadow economy. Therefore, many studies found that social security contribution has a positive impact on the size of shadow economy (Schneider et al., 2010 and Schneider, 1994a, 1994b, 2005, 2007). Social transfer is also investigated by Lemieux et al. (1994) and Schneider and Enste (2000) and they found a direct relationship between social transfer and shadow economy, as such payment discourages people from working in official economy, while for additional income they will join shadow economy.

3.2 Intensity of Regulations

The main purpose of imposition of rules and regulations, on one hand, is to make markets socially and economically justifiable, enhance social welfare, redistribute wealth in a correct way, and decrease external influences, while on the other hand, it is to solve market problems and save markets from failure. Similarly, rules and regulations are made to provide protection for labor. But at one point in time, such regulations create a problem and people start to consider such regulations as a barrier to their social and economic freedom. Whereas, on firms' level, fulfilling rules and regulations increases the cost of production and brings additional costs.

32 Main Causal Factors of Shadow Economy

If such regulations become extensive, then the impact becomes even worse and opens the door to corruption, specifically in developing nations (Schneider, 2000). Therefore, both at the individual and the firm levels, intensity of regulations are barriers to freedom and a source of increase in cost of production respectively. Frey and Weck-Hannemann (1984) found that the basic push behind participating in shadow economy is the regulations in official economy.

According to Schneider (2004), one of the important causes of shadow economy is the intensity of regulations and the reduction of the freedom of businesses and individuals to participate in formal economy, which are proxied by license necessities and number of laws. Similarly, Johnson et al. (1997) find that the percentage of shadow economy will be higher for a country having more market regulations. Other scholars like Friedman et al. (2000) see interesting results: there is a strong connection between shadow economy and regulation, where shadow economy is increased by 10% with an increase in one point in index of regulation. The imposition and implementation of regulations on individuals and businesses are the main factors for joining shadow economy Johnson et al. (1998a), and the failure of the government to provide satisfactory regulations may cause individuals and businesses to switch toward shadow economy (Risteski, 2016).

3.3 Public Sector Service

One of the main responsibilities of government is to provide public goods and services like defense, infrastructure, and so on. Therefore, the provision of public goods and services depends on the revenue generated by the government through different sources like taxes, fees, and other types of duties. But one way or the other, upsurge in shadow economy creates a hurdle in the way of providing public services, as it reduces government revenue. Such reduction in revenue compels government to increase and expend taxation and other fees so as to overcome the budget deficit. Such increase in taxation creates a vicious cycle of throwing more people in the shadow economy. Therefore, the role of the public sector cannot be ignored in the discussion of causal factors of shadow economy (Schneider et al., 2010).

So, the decision of increasing or imposing additional taxes, as well as other public services costs, should be properly analyzed before implementation; otherwise, it will lead to a vicious cycle because an increase in tax rates and other public charges will lead to a rise in shadow economy more by throwing additional people to the shadow economy, which will further decrease public service quality and revenue from taxation and will end in further reduction in government revenue. So, the vicious cycle will continue if government goes with the same policies, but on the other hand the vicious cycle can be changed into a virtuous cycle if government puts forward the right policies (Schneider and Williams, 2013). Countries that have fewer rules and regulations, and a low rate of taxation, are found to have a small size of shadow and vice versa (Johnson et al., 1998a).

3.4 Official Economy

It is one of the core objectives of any government to boost economic growth and bring prosperity to the country. But many studies (Feld and Schneider, 2010 and Schneider and Enste, 2000) cite the decision of citizens to operate in shadow economy or not, have very close links with official economy growth and development. If the formal economy develops with a rapid growth rate, it will bring incentive to the businesses and entrepreneurs to operate in formal sector, as the businesses are getting good return while the workers are getting good compensation. But in case of the inverse situation, where official economy is facing downfall, people will look for shadow economy to recompense a decrease in returns (Schneider et al., 2010).

One of the main issues with shadow economy is that the factors of productions and other economic and human resources implied in shadow economy are not utilized in an efficient way. If the shadow economy boosts, it will attract entrepreneurs and laborers from the formal economy to the shadow economy in order to benefit from reducing the cost of production because of facing fewer regulations. To summarize, shadow economic activities create competition for the workers and businesses, which are operated in the formal sector of the economy. Along with this negative effect on official economy, there is a positive impact as well, where two-thirds of the income generated in shadow economy is spent in formal economy, which boosts aggregate demand (AD) as a result leads to more production and goods and services in official economy (Schneider and Enste, 2013).

Surprisingly, education spending is found to increase shadow economy (Torgler et al., 2010). Similarly, it is found by Ott (1998) that unproductive expenditure of government leads to upsurge shadow economy by accumulation of additional taxes from masses which unswervingly push them towards shadow economy.

3.5 Unemployment

One of the main causal factors of shadow economy is unemployment. Schneider (2005) found that the size of shadow economy in a developing economy (38.7%) and transition (40.1%) are high as compared to advanced (16.3%) nations. According to him, there are many factors behind such higher size of shadow economy, especially in developing nations. Along with others, unemployment is one of them, because in developing economy growth rate is normally slow as compared to their population growth. As a result, the government fails to produce employment opportunities for all labor force in the economy. Therefore, a substantial portion of labor force join shadow economy. Second, the official sector normally needs skilled, experienced, and educated workers, while in developing economies all these things are lacking.

Therefore, there are no opportunities for them to directly join official sector because of a lack of required skills and training, social connections, and documentation that are required to have occupations in official economy. Some of these workers are illegal migrants who are receiving salaries below minimum wage.

34 *Main Causal Factors of Shadow Economy*

Similarly, many skillful workers operate in shadow economy because of getting more wages as compared to official economy. Finally, a shadow economy can be chosen by some labors because of enjoying flexibility in working hours and so on (Hall, 2017). According to Ela (2013), due to a lack of skill and education in workers who migrated to urban areas from rural areas, they are unable to find employment in official sector. Therefore, in order to sustain their livelihoods, they join shadow economy. The developing countries are not able to create employment for low-educated and unskilled workers; therefore, they remain unemployed and then move to shadow economy. These workers are costly for official sector proprietors, therefore they are compelled to work in shadow economy.

4 Empirical Scholarship on Shadow Economy

Before explaining the main theories of shadow economy, first we need to investigate the empirical work in the context of shadow economy. Therefore, this chapter covers empirical scholarship on shadow economy such as empirical literature on the determinants of shadow economy, empirical literature on financial development and shadow economy, and empirical literature on financial inclusion and shadow economy.

4.1 Empirical Literature on the Determinants of Shadow Economy

Under the empirical literature, we examine literature on the determinants of shadow economy. Similarly, we also look upon literature on financial development and shadow economy and finally literature on the role of financial inclusion on shadow economy has been assessed. Empirically speaking, whether shadow economy is good or bad for the economy is controversial and conflicting. Some scholars like Schneider et al. (2003) for Asian countries, Giles and Tedds (2002) and Tedds (2005) for Canada, and Adam and Ginsburgh (1985) for Belgium find shadow economy to be good for the economy. Other scholars, for instance Dell'Anno et al. (2007) for France, Greece, and Spain; Dell'Anno (2003) for Italy; Ott (2002) for Croatia; Frey and Weck-Hanneman (1984) for 17 OECD countries; Kaufmann and Kaliberda (1996) for transition countries; Schneider and Enste (2000) for 76 countries, and Eilat and Zinnes (2000) for transition countries explore shadow economy to be an evil for economy. Some established shadow economy to be positive for advanced nations while harmful for developing and transition economies.

Therefore, there are too many divergences in worldwide literature regarding shadow economy (ILO, 2013a), as well as at national (Williams, 2014; Putniņš and Sauka, 2015; Papyrakis, 2014; Schneider, 2013 and Likic-Brboric et al., 2013), regional, and local levels (Williams and Shahid, 2016 and Kesteltoot and Meert, 1999). Similarly, deviations are found in different income groups (Boels, 2014 and Williams, 2004), employment situations (Williams et al., 2013), age groups (Pedersen, 2003), and finally different gender categories (ILO, 2013a; Leonard, 1994, 1998 and Stănculescu, 2005).

DOI: 10.4324/9781003329954-4

36 *Empirical Scholarship on Shadow Economy*

There are numerous studies regarding the estimation of the size of shadow economy, but one of the famous studies is conducted by Schneider (2005) while studying 145 economies from all over the world. He divides the economies into three major groups: advanced, transition, and developing nations and finds the size of shadow economy in developing nations is 38.7%, transition is 40.1%, and advanced is 16.3% respectively.

Bearing in mind that most of the under-investigation economies are developing countries and the size of shadow economy in OIC economies is 34.36% and non-OIC economies is 30.57%. Therefore, this large size of shadow economy should be considered while having economic policies for an economy. Because if there is an interaction between shadow economy and formal economy, the resulted impact on a country's socioeconomic factors will be positive (Naidoo, 2002 and ILO, 1993) while in contrast, growth rate of an economy will reduce if government policies support shadow economy (Walker and Wade, 2011 and Ranieri and Almeida Ramos, 2013). Similarly, some studies claim positive relationship of shadow economy with formal economy (Becker, 2004 and Arias and Khamis, 2008) where more government revenue will enable the government to enhance expenditure on public goods and services and will result in low shadow economy.

Becker (2004) and Arias and Khamis (2008) confirmed that there is an incentive to connect with shadow economy, because of relatively higher profit expectation. So, if the profit rate of shadow economy is relatively superior to formal sector, then more numbers of individuals will penetrate into shadow economy. Legalist school of thought also recognizes bureaucracy, that is, complexity in registration is an important factor for the growth of shadow economy (Chen et al., 2004). Economic crisis brings adverse effects to the economy, that is, people losing jobs, collapse in business, and aggregate demand declines, and incentivized to go for the shadow economy to earn livelihood and get some extra economic benefits (Chen,2012). Some studies find positive association between shadow economy and cash in circulation because usually cash and high denominated notes are used for transaction in shadow economic activities, in order to escape from tracing by government (Bawly, 1982; Feige, 2003 and Kaur, 2016).

Economic growth is considered one of the main indicators of people's well-being. Therefore, the determinants of economic growth have been studied for many years by using different time spans, aspects, and space (Mankiw, Romer and Weil, 1992.and Barro and Sala-i-Martin, 2003). While shadow economy is the second economy along with official economy, which not only has connection with official economy but at the same time also has substantial impact on economic growth. Therefore, shadow economy attracts a lot of researchers and economists to see its determinants and effects (Schneider and Enste, 2000), but because of issues regarding its measurement, the empirical research is quite new.

In the last decades, researchers have given considerable attention to the shadow economy in advanced and transition countries. But there are few studies on developing economies, especially in the context of OIC member states.

Empirical Scholarship on Shadow Economy   37

Studies concerning transition as well as developing economies have been explored, for instance, applying currency demand model and using date period from 1976 to 2002, Schneider and Hametner (2014) described that in Colombia, the main driving forces of shadow economy are taxes and unemployment, while the size of shadow economy rises from 20% of GDP in the 1970s to 50% of GDP in the 1990s. While studying shadow economy and tax gap in Brazil, Lucinda and Arvate (2005) indicate that shadow economy has increased at the time of imposition of Provisional Contribution on Financial Transactions, or CPMF, and CPMF are responsible for such increase. Similarly, the total loss from shadow economy is counted as 2046 million reais at the study period (1995–2002). Applying currency demand approach while using data spanning from 1983 to 2003, Asiedu and Stengos (2014) focus on shadow economy in Ghana and exhibited that, in 1985, the size of shadow economy was as high as 54% while in 1999 it was as low as 25% and in the long run, the average size of shadow economy remains 40%.

Siddiki (2014) uses real GDP per capita growth, tax revenue, import and export, as well as government spending for Bangladesh in 1999–2005. and applies MIMIC model. The range of shadow economy came out to be 13.47% in 1984 to 37% in 2010, where monetization has negative and tax has positive impact on shadow economy. Recently, Hassan and Schneider (2016) investigated shadow economy in Egypt and used a long data period, from 1976–2013. They applied both currency demand and MIMIC models and have examined declining slope of the size of shadow economy from 50% in 1976 to 32% in 2013. Despite continued downward trend, the percentage is still convincing.

Chaudhuri et al. (2006) studied shadow economy in 14 different states of India from 1974–1995 applying MIMIC model. They brought an interesting result: that after liberalization in 1991, shadow economy has decreased because of rising literacy rates and growth in newspapers circulation. While in election years, the size of shadow economy has been 4%, which is less than compared to other years. According to Neuwirth (2011), in Nigeria and China, there is too much application of informal sector to the official sector producers and suppliers.

Arby et al. (2010) find that the size of shadow economy in Pakistan is 30% by using MIMIC approach, while Tan et al. (2016) study the shadow economy in Malaysia by using autoregressive distributed lag (ARDL) approach and indicate that there is an inverse relationship between income and shadow economy while burden of tax pushes upward shadow economy. In the same way unemployment impact on shadow economy is positive. Another attempt has been made by Bourhaba and Mama (2016) to estimate the size of shadow economy in Morocco by using data period from 1999 to 2015 and have applied MIMIC model. The result indicates that the size of shadow economy is 42.9% of the GDP in 2015, while there is upward propensity and growth in the size of shadow economy. The main players they have explored are increase in rate of urbanization, tax burden, and increase in corruption. By using a household survey Albu (2008) has studied the informal economy and revealed that deprived classes of society are participating in shadow economy for survival motives.

38 *Empirical Scholarship on Shadow Economy*

4.2 Empirical Literature on Financial Development and Shadow Economy

There is some tiny work on the relationship of financial development with shadow economy. Berdiev and Saunoris (2016) investigate the impact of financial development on shadow economy by using panel vector auto-regression model and data spanning from 1960 to 2009. They find that financial development reduces shadow economy. In the case of Italy, Capasso and Jappelli (2013) also indicate that financial development reduces shadow economy and tax evasion. By applying Maki (2012) cointegration test in Turkey and using data spanning from 1960 to 2009, Bayar and Aytemiz (2017) discover that in the long run financial development reduces the size of shadow economy and the direction of causality is only from financial development to shadow economy. Another study by Din et al. (2016) for Malaysia, using data spanning from 1971 to 2013, estimates the size of shadow economy by applying the modified cash deposits ratio technique and expose inverted U shape (nonlinear) relationship between shadow economy and financial development. They signify that at initial stage financial development increases shadow economy but as the financial sector grows further, shadow economy decreases. In order to reduce shadow economy, availability of credit and improving financing system have key roles.

Elgin and Uras (2013) present the connection between financial development and shadow economy and identify that because of creating financial suppression by evading taxes, shadow economy is hurtful for financial development. Conversely, shadow economy is beneficial to financial sector because of enabling the size restriction of financial sector. Similarly, the connection among quality of institutions, shadow economy, and financial development have been evaluated in European Union transition countries using time from 2003 to 2014 by applying panel data technique. The result shows that both quality of institutions and financial development reduce shadow economy in the long run (Bayar and Ozturk, 2016). Blackburn et al. (2012) conclude that individuals will be willing to disclose their wealth with the development of financial markets, and the size of shadow economy will be large, if the stage of such development is low.

Hosseini et al. (2014) investigate the impact of financial development and monetary development on the size of shadow economy in Iran by using data period 1973 to 2009 and applying ARDL technique. They predict that shadow economy decreases as monetary and financial development increases. According to Djankov et al. (2002), the economies that have onerous entrance regulations and rules are found to have a larger size of shadow economy. Bose et al. (2012) explore the association between shadow economy and banking sector development by using data spanning from 1995 to 2007 for 137 economies and applying panel and cross-sectional techniques. They propose negative impact of banking sector development on shadow economy. In order to reduce shadow economy, both efficiency and depth of the banking sector are crucial. By using Arellano-Bond Generalized Method of Moments technique (GMM) on 20 European Union countries between 2006 and 2014, Imamoglu (2017) explains that financial development significantly impacts shadow economy. He also finds that GDP and shadow economy are inversely correlated.

The benefits to the firms to go underground have been investigated by Dabla-Norris et al. (2008) where they have collected data from 41 countries and have utilized 4,000 registered units operating in shadow economy. They reveal that there is a 16% probability of hiding their 50% sales for those firms who consider financing as the key obstacle. The firms that consider financing is a slight barrier, have a probability of 7.6% to hide their sales. Gatti and Honorati (2008) find that having less avoidance of taxes brings more access to credit. They have used data from investment climate surveys at firms' level from 49 countries. In the same fashion, La Porta and Shleifer (2008) predict that there is a strong connection between private credit and shadow economy. Likewise, by using data period of 1980–2009 for 150 economies, Bittencourt et al. (2014) conclude that the size of shadow economy rises with high inflation rates and low level of financial development. In the latest study, Berdiev and Saunoris (2016) disclose that the impact of financial development on shadow economy is negative. They also found converse causality where shadow economy reduces financial development. They have used dynamic panel technique (VAR) for 161 countries and their data spans from 1960 to 2009.

4.3 Empirical Literature on Financial Inclusion and Shadow Economy

In this section, shadow economy has been seen from the perspective of financial inclusion. Financial inclusion is defined as the shares and portions of firms that utilize and practice financial facilities and services or "a process that ensures the ease of access, availability and usage of the formal financial system for all members of an economy". In the preceding definitions, there are three main terms: usage, access, and availability of official financial system. In the global world today, according to IFC (2012), 80% of medium, micro, and small businesses (MMSEs) are operating in shadow economy while 1.8 billion people are working in shadow economy (OECD, 2009). Similarly, according to World Bank, access to credit and finance is the main hurdle for the firms who are operating in the shadow economy. The firms that are operating in the shadow economy are facing several problems, which are badly affecting their processes and development. Some of these problems have association with public sector like land, water, and power, which may be due to low quality of institutions or less advantages in operating in official sector, that is, access to financing, technology (Farazi, 2014).[1]

Utilizing data from 2000 to 2005, Nastav and Bojnec (2008) studied two-sided correlation between shadow economy and small businesses in ten EU new member countries. Their results suggest that privatization, deregulation, and free market economy are the sources and bring novel breaks for new sources of revenue, entrepreneurs, and small businesses, while on the other hand, costly institutions, strict regulations, and high taxation are the drivers to push people toward shadow

40   *Empirical Scholarship on Shadow Economy*

economy. The development of quality institutions and better macroeconomics fundamentals delaying shadow economy and inspiring businesses. Capasso and Jappelli (2013) study shadow economy relation with finance in Italy and exhibited that local financial development is negatively correlated with shadow economy. While shedding light on the importance of micro, small, and medium businesses, Farazi (2014) predicts that the firms operating in shadow economy are utilizing very low-level bank accounts and loans for financing their business operations. Instead of financial institutions, they are using other sources like family, friends, internal capitals, and moneylenders. Payment of taxes are the main hurdle for formalization of these firms, otherwise they would like to join official economy. The likeliness to have access to funds is 54% and to a bank account is 32% for the firms who are recorded with the government. Proprietor education level, having a job in official sector or not, and the size of the firm have significantly close connection of informal firms with financial inclusion.

By utilizing Italian credit market panel data, Gobbi and Zizza (2007) expose inverse impact on credit to private sector of informal employment. A switching of 1% from formal to informal employment leads to decrease of 0.3% credit to private sector and 0.2% size of business lending. The 2002 initiative of informal emigrants' labors formalization, they also detect those informal workers who hurdle for bank decisions to participate in the local credit market. Examining pilot data from Fin-Scope Surveys, De Koker and Jentzsch (2013) study eight African countries and show that there is no guarantee that informal services will inevitably be reduced with growth in access to formal services utilization, particularly, in a situation where people are using informal financing along with formal facilities. Lack of transparency in the formal financial system is creating the main hurdle to use formal financial services and are keeping away people and businesses from integration and financial inclusion.

To summarize, it is well-known that most of the OIC economies are developing, and one of the important issues in developing economies regarding formulating economic policies is the nonexistence of efficient, timely, accurate, reliable, and consistent data on one hand while on the other hand there is a huge portion of shadow economy, that is, 34.36% in OIC states, which is not recognized in national statistics. Even though national statistics are available and in line with the national account system, still it deteriorates in terms of inaccuracy and deficiency of valuation of economic variables and economic activities. Similarly, in these countries, data collection is problematic and estimation methods suffer from deficiency. In these countries, firms and businesses keep information secret from government authorities because of involvement in illicit and shadow activities. Authenticity and accuracy of economic statistics and data are important to implement and formulate efficient and effective economic policies and allocate resources in a proper way. So, if the size of shadow economy is large, it creates governance problems, signaling the presence of excessive regulations, understates national income and other macroeconomic variables. If macroeconomic variables present wrong information, then the policies based on such variables will also be incorrect and inefficient.

It can also be concluded that shadow economy exists in all types of economies in different shapes and in unlikely places. Many researchers and economists have studied shadow economy from different perspectives by using different methodologies and achieving distinct objectives because of the complex, dynamic, and heterogeneity of present-day economies (Becker, 2004 and Schneider, 2005). However, characteristics, nature, determinants, and size of shadow economy differ from country to country. Researchers have studied shadow economy in advanced and transaction countries while less concentration has been given to developing countries. As we have realized in the aforementioned literature, there is a knowledge gap regarding shadow economy in the context of OIC countries; we find lack of work regrading determinants of shadow economy while the role of financial development and financial inclusion in shadow economy are missing in the literature especially in OIC countries.

The preceding stated empirical research works are conflicting regarding main determinants of shadow economy. It may be due to differences in time periods, methodologies they have used, and variances in the nature of economies, that is, developed, emerging, developing, and low-income economies. On the other hand, a majority of the studies found negative association between financial inclusion and shadow economy. Finally, there is a lack of literature on the association between financial inclusion and shadow economy. This study approaches the issue of shadow economy from different angles in order to fill the gap in the literature. There is an important contribution of this work because the value added by this work will open the door for the future research in this ignored but important part of the economy, especially in OIC member countries.

Note

1 IFC (International Finance Corporation). 2012. Enterprise Finance Gap Database. World Bank, Washington DC.

5 Theories of Shadow Economy

There are many concerns about the rise and presence of shadow economy but three of them need serious consideration. First, shadow economy's activities are hidden from official record, which causes tax loss to the government. Second, the presence of shadow economy is an indication of unsound relationship between government and public. People become part of the shadow economy if they are unsatisfied with the services they receive from government vis-à-vis their tax contribution. Thus, it creates problems for the government in terms of financing projects and development expenses by losing tax revenue. Third, the picture of social and economic situation of people, in particular, and the whole economy, in general, is displayed inaccurately if only official facts and figures are considered. Hence, the labor who work in shadow economy are considered unemployed in the official record, but in fact they are rewarded and receive income. This situation results in expansionary macroeconomic policies and extra social benefits and security expenses (Frey and Schneider, 2000).

One of the causes for the scarcity of empirical research work on shadow economy is the paucity of theoretical foundation and framework that provide theoretical justification and explanation of the behavior and nature of shadow economy. It is due to the fact that theoretical foundation is the base for explaining any economic phenomenon. It also provides foundation for empirical research. However, due to lack of theories, empirical research explaining the behavior of shadow economy is scarce (ILO, 1972; De Soto, 1989 and Portes et al., 1989). Taking into consideration the importance of theoretical background, in this chapter we explain different theories of shadow economy so as to get a deeper understanding of this phenomenon. The different theories and schools that could be figured out about shadow economy include Dualist, Structuralist, Legalist, and Voluntarist schools as well as Complementary Theory, Illegalist Thought, Inclusionist Perspective, the Modern Perspective, and shadow economy theories application to OIC countries.

5.1 The Dualist School

This school considers shadow economy totally isolated from formal economy without any connection between the two. According to this school, shadow

DOI: 10.4324/9781003329954-5

economy provides shelter, survival, and a safety net to the poor people, and at the same time it is a source of income for the deprived segment of society. In their view, shadow economy is the consequence of downfall in economic growth and development, whereby the economy fails to accommodate all labor force (ILO, 1972). Specifically, in the developing world, the informal activities are marginalized and isolated from the official economy. The informal activities arise from the contribution of negligence and low-income people's participation in economic activities. Thus, on the one hand is a source of income for them and on the other hand it provides a safeguard against any economic downfall or crisis.

The stance of Dualist school mainly supports the stages of economic growth; huge and large size of shadow economy is a sign of less employment and business opportunities where developing economy is not able to provide job and business breaks to all active and desirous population. It is due to two reasons: first, the economic growth is slow to absorb all labor force. Second, the less developing economies have high population growth as compared to employment opportunities which creates the problem of providing jobs to all of them. In support of its opinion, this school brings arguments from the perspective of recession and expansion of economy. They argue that in case of slowdown of an economy, shadow economy is a place of storage and a safety net that provides employment and business chance to the labor force and entrepreneurs. Once the economy grows, it returns back the labor force to official economy. Shadow economy is appreciated for its contribution in terms of providing cheap goods and services for the poor to sustain their relationship with society. In addition, with the introduction of industrialization, the world economies grow faster than before, while the shadow economy is found to decrease with the increasing economic development of nations (Bhattacharyya, 2009).

In most of the developing countries, the system of production and distribution of goods and services, especially in urban areas, are dual. Therefore, Sethuraman (1976, 1981) distinguishes formal and informal economies on the bases of their characteristics like how production and distribution of goods and services take place in both formal sector and informal sector. In the middle of the twentieth century, Geertz (1963, 1978) spots dualism in rural economic activities in Indonesia and identifies "bazaar sector" and "firm-centered sector". He observes that economic activities are taking place in traditional markets, called *Pasar*. Such a market is a type of economic activities center and is joined by all people for commercial purposes. Micro level production and distribution of goods and services are taking place in that market where business activities happen one-to one. In such a market, a substantial quantity of negligent individuals is engaged. He also observes a sort of organized type of economic doings in Modjokuto, a small market town in East Central Java, which are closer to firm-type economic activities as compared to bazaar type. The economic activities of such an economy are in order, organized, systematic, and greater scale. The distribution of economic activities into "firm-centered sector" and "bazaar sector" gives us a clear picture to understand economic dualism specially in developing world.

44 Theories of Shadow Economy

In our study, most of the OIC economies are developing and the expected distribution of their economies into two segments is not far away, where informal economy can grow and cultivate its seeds along with formal economy. Since the beginning, the concept of duality exists between formal sector and informal sector (ILO, 1972 and Hart, 1973). Even the pioneer of this area, Keith Hart, is also inclined toward the Dualist school of thought, which considers shadow economy as in autonomous and isolated sector from formal economy. The informal economic activities have been studied by many scholars, especially in low-income countries. But their stance on informal economy is different from one another. Scholars like Mazumdar (1976), Dannhaeuser (1977), Langdon (1975), Kaplinsky (1979), Bromley (1978), Birkbeck (1979), Gerry and Birkbeck (1981), Banerjee (1983), Young and Moser (1981), Moser (1978), Norcliffe (1983), and Bolnick (1992) consider it totally reliant, lethargic, and producing weightless revenue to contribute to the overall economy. According to these scholars, informal economic activities have nothing to do with a country's development; these are producing tiny incomes, exploiting on the basis of gender, wasting country resources, are problematic to the public and have a static nature in terms of technology, finance, markets, and raw materials while hampering the capital of participants.

There exists a contrary school of thought: ILO (1972), King (1974), Merrick (1976), Jellinek (1978), Nihan and Jourdain (1978), Nihan et al. (1979), Baxter (1980), McGee et al. (1980), Walsh (1982), Beavon and Roger (1982), and Teilhet-Waldorf and Waldorf (1983). Some writers have also emphasized ways of improving the welfare of informal sector activities and its participants. These writers present their propositions in a way to support and look at the positive aspects of informal economy. They argue that shadow economy plays a very important role in the economic growth of a country in general, while it provides an income source to individuals in specific in order to sustain their livelihoods. They bring solid proposition by mentioning that shadow economy is observed by providing successful career and income growth for poor people who are the major participants in this sector. Shadow economy supports participants in terms of developing their skills at an initial level and offers the opportunity to have experience before joining official or big industry. It is a place of training where individuals use minor technology that is suitable for their jobs and businesses at the local level. These individuals then implement such skill in the broader development of the economy. It is the informal sector that performs a significant part in the reduction of income inequality on one hand while boosting circulation of wealth as well as redistribution of country resources on the other (Tokman, 1978, 1989; Khundker, 1988; Chandavarkar, 1988; Levenson and Maloney, 1998 and Dasgupta, 2003).

Unlike the "bazaar" and "firm-centered" proposition of Geertz (1963) and the "formal" and "informal" proposition of ILO (1972) and Hart (1973), Santos (1977) proposes the notion of "upper" and "lower" which he calls the "circuits" of production and distribution. According to Santos (1977), there are two circuits (upper and lower) of employment in third-world economies, which exist simultaneously but differ in mode of production of goods and services where the upper circuit dominates the lower. Santos' major contribution to the area is that

Theories of Shadow Economy 45

he finds that there is a dynamic link between upper and lower circuits while such relationship is reciprocal in nature to the production and distribution of goods and services. Santos is different from other scholars of the area, as he discusses the linkage and relationship between the two systems. So, the work of Santos reduces the gap in academic thought of this area of knowledge by conceptualizing economics activities of Third World countries in terms of duality.

Another proportion has been presented by Marxists and Dependency theorists via the notion of "mode of production" for urban economic activities where they name informal sector as "petty commodity production". The "petty commodity production" is used while referring to economic activities that are "outside the major axis of capitalist production and/or market relations" (Bechhofer and Elliott, 1981: p. 123). According to this theory, petty commodity production is "a distinct economic form, found in the context of several modes of production (feudal, capitalist or socialist) Petty commodity production is normally subordinate, dependent and transitional" (Bechhofer and Elliott, 1981: p. 128). Dependency and Marxist authors term the link between big capitalist businesses and petty commodity production as "petty commodity bourgeoisie", where local bourgeoisie provide funds, market, and resources to petty commodity bourgeoisie to grow and develop their businesses. Despite the cooperation of national bourgeoisie, majority petty commodity producers' income remains static and even declines, and the minor producers generate income to sustain livelihood (Bromley and Gerry, 1979; Gerry and Birkbeck, 1981 and Forbes, 1981). All this discussion points toward connection of petty commodity production and development of capitalism (Gerry and Birkbeck, 1981).

According to Nattress (1987), informal sector is labor intensive and has capital constraint. Informal sector produces goods and services outside the domain of official economy because of low production standard and business licensing and documentation costs. Similarly, informal sector of developing economies has been studied by Jagannathan (1987) and who has found that in Africa and Asia poor people have property rights even though these rights may not contribute to them in the form of income source. With the help of informal contracts, these poor people have access to property rights in formal economy. Thus, he found some sort of connection of petty businesses in the shadow economy with official economy. It should be noted that even though petty commodity production is dynamic, and competition based, it is not dualistic like "upper" and "lower", "formal" and "informal", as well as "bazaar" and "firm-centered".

Another proposition is presented recently by Levenson and Maloney (1998) and Maloney (2004), which suggests that it is unsuitable to study informal sector through traditional Dualistic approach. They studied the economic behavior of people in informal sector in Latin America and Mexico and found different models like employees working on wage; employees working on percentage, commission, or fixed-base contracts; self-employed; informal firms' proprietors with and without extra workers; and so on. They find one common feature in all; they have frequent association with large firms of the official economy. They observe a high level of heterogeneous behavior in shadow economy. Surprisingly, Dualistic labor

46   *Theories of Shadow Economy*

market has nothing to do with people's decision, and they join informal economy by their own choice.

Even though informal sector is heterogeneous having dynamic characteristics and connections with official economy, still it is not able to grow and develop. There are many factors that create barriers to the growth of informal sector, like the huge difference between salaries of formal and informal sector workers. Similarly, the cost of capital for informal sector is relatively high; likewise, charging high interest on credit and financing to informal sector is another reason. The supply chain of informal products through formal sector are seen as one of the main hurdles to the growth and development of informal sector. The mutual effect of these factors prevents informal workers and businesses to boost and develop (Hemmer and Mannel, 1989; Chaudhuri, 1989 and Dasgupta, 2003).

To conclude, the Dualist proposition considers shadow economy isolated from official economy; at the time of recession, it provides a safety net and a source of income; in the case of economic expansion, it returns back the labor force with experience and skill. One school considers it a waste of resources, providing tiny income, problematic to the public, and having nothing to do with a country's development. Others say that it plays an important role in economic growth by providing cheaper goods and services, careers, experience, skills, and income opportunities.

It also reduces income inequality, boosts circulation of wealth, and redistributes a country's resources. Shadow economy is a place of training where individuals use minor technology that is suitable for their jobs and businesses at the local level. Later, they implement such skill in broader development of the economy. Relatively low salaries, high cost of capital, high interest rate, and difficulty in supply chain are the main barriers to the growth of shadow economy. Shadow economy is labor intensive and capital constraint sector. It produces goods and services outside the domain of official economy as its production standard is low and not able to compete with official businesses. It is also not capable to bear business licensing and documentation costs. The people in informal sector have property rights in official economy even though these rights may not contribute to them in form of income source. Finally, with the introduction of industrialization, the economies of the world grow faster than before while the shadow economy is found to be decreased with increasing economic development of world nations.

Thus, it is clearly apparent from the preceding discussion that during recession time, shadow economy expands, and at the time of economic growth, it shrinks. So, the first recommendation is to increase production level and economic growth. This can be done through financial development, as it is the engine for economic growth. Second, the barrier from the supply chain of informal sector should be removed, which can be done through connection of unofficial economy with formal sector. Third, increasing standard of production in informal sector is required, which can be done through moderating standard of production in official economy to merge them together and conducting awareness program regarding production process. Fourth, reduction in cost of businesses registration and documentation is needed, which can be done through quality of institutions and promotion of business-friendly environment. Fifth, there should be a reduction in the cost of capital for informal sector through financial inclusion. Here Islamic banking comes in to play a role in OIC countries. Seventh, access to funds should be facilitated via financial development. In this regard, Islamic financial institutions come in to play a role, especially in OIC economies. Eighth, interest rates should be reduced through Islamic economic system, which is interest free.

5.2 The Structuralist/Dependency School

The proposition of this school of thought is that both formal and informal sectors are closely connected, and informal firms and businesses are just secondary to a big firm in official sector. Thus, this school defines shadow economy as a combination of all revenue generating economic activities where goods and services are produced which are not regulated by the government within social surroundings (Castells and Portes, 1989). Considering this definition, shadow economy is not only associated with developing nations, it also covers current advanced, post-industrial revolution, and postmodern sectors of the economy. Because this definition looks at the broader picture, it is totally different from the previous one and considers shadow economy as a subordinate to the official economy.

The main argument is that large firms in the official sector reduce cost of production with the association of shadow sector while big firms exist everywhere in the world regardless of developing countries and developed nations. Therefore, this definition opens room for shadow economy to exist in advanced nations too. As Portes and Sassen-Koob (1987) have evaluated shadow economy from the perspective of industrial development theories, they have assessed shadow economy characteristics, activities, dynamics, and growth and development. They have found that in shadow economy there is no clear division between money and labor, where laborers work and get rewards without proper contract and agreement. The market transaction takes place but there are not clear contractual obligations upon buyer and seller. But it is known and has a diversified nature like small firms and companies, low level of production, survival, and house-based workers and small businesses.

Similarly, they have proposed that the institutions, political condition, and history of a country make some structures more plausible than others in which shadow economy is a subordinate of official economy. In order to become more competitive by reducing cost (labor cost and capital cost) of production, firms and businesses in the official economy subordinate small producers and traders in the shadow economy (Portes et al., 1989). In order to merge informal sector with official economy, political environment and institutional setting should be reformed accordingly. They comment that most of the developing countries markets are incomplete and inefficient that are not capable to move to the full employment equilibrium level, thus incompleteness of the markets gives way to shadow economy existence and growth.

According to Castells and Portes (1989), unregistered sector is a subsidiary part that consists of small firms and labors, which is part of big capitalist firms for

48 *Theories of Shadow Economy*

achieving reduction in cost of production. In contrast to Dualist view, this model considers production and distribution of goods and services interdependent and highly correlated between formal and informal sectors, while distinction on the basis of production and trading procedures. The informal sector exists not because of lack of economic growth and development, it is the capitalist model itself that gives way to unofficial sector production process, growth and development unlike Dualist school which brings arguments from the perspective of size of the firm, social and economic position of the employees, kind of economic activities, characteristics of the businesses and workers, and finally the total amount of capital financing (Portes and Sassen-Koob, 1987; Castells and Portes, 1989; Benton, 1989; Fernández-Kelly and Garcia, 1989; Sassen-Koob, 1989 and Sassen, 1994).

In summary, we can say that in order to reduce cost of production and to become more competitive, big firms from the official sector subordinate small suppliers and producers in the shadow economy. According to classical economists, full employment can be achieved if all resources are utilized but the developing nations due to incompleteness and inefficiency in the market, are always below full employment, which opens a door not only to the existence of shadow economy but also its growth and development. They consider both sectors interdependent and closely connected, but they differ from each other in terms of the way they deal and produce goods and services. In order to justify the existence of shadow economy in advanced nations, they argue that big firms in the official sector reduce cost of production with the coordination of informal economy while these large firms exist everywhere in the world, especially in developed nations which validate the existence of shadow economy also in developed countries. The empirical studies also support this proposition as the famous study conducted by Schneider (2005) finds that shadow economy in transition countries is 40.1% and in highly advanced nations is 16.3% as a percentage of official GDP respectively.

5.3 The Legalist/Neoliberal School

This school of thought emerged in the late 1980s, propagated by Hernando de Soto with the proposition that shadow economy is a response to overregulation (Chen et al., 2004). According to De Soto (1989), with the intention of evading business registration costs, saving time and effort, "plucky" micro businesses decide to function in shadow economy. According to this school, shadow economy is a reaction to the overregulation in official economy. It has become almost impossible for the micro, small, and medium enterprises to follow the complicated regulations and bureaucratic procedures of government. Therefore, in order to avoid such regulations and procedures, these firms operate in the shadow economy where they can reduce cost of production and increase income and wealth creation. De Soto is a supporter of classical school of economics and suggests no government (laissez-faire) intervention in economic life of people. His arguments are based on the idea that, initially, it is created by the government because of too much intervention in the economy in the form of overregulation. Both shadow economy and inflated regulations are mutually exhaustive, which means

Theories of Shadow Economy 49

that shadow economy and excessive regulations both will exist at the same time. Whenever there is overregulation, shadow economy will always be there. He further pronounces that informal businesses and workers seek shelter in shadow economy from burdensome government documentations. De Soto (1989: p. 255) states that "the real problem is not so much informality as formality" meaning that it is too many formalities that bring informality.

From the preceding discussion, we can conclude that De Soto is the proponent of neoliberal school who is more inclined toward classical school who are in favor of no government intervention in economic activities. Supply and demand forces will adjust to equilibrium with the support of an invisible hand. Second, from a pure economics perspective, we can say that it is the government fiscal policy that have crowded out some businesses and thrown them in the shadow economy, as these businesses have not been able to compete with them in the official economy.

It is beneficial to the lower classes of society to stay away from the domain of official economy and reduce cost of doing business (Willman-Navarro, 2008). So, shadow economy is the response of deprived class of society to the failure of government to fulfill their economic needs and provide efficient services concerning business registrations (De Soto, 1989).

The desire of every economy is to grow rich and make advancement. Shadow sector is that part of economy that provides pushup to the economy, engine to the equalized demand and supply forces, and correct the unbalance behavior of economic fundamentals of an economy. The De Soto focus is to take care of deprived part of the society and provide basic source of income should be the main objective of every country. The resource distribution among rich and poor should be equal, otherwise the poor will be deprived further on the one hand and the rich will grow richer on the other hand. As a result, inequality will waste further, ensuring social unrest and injustice. Thus, the main proposition of this school of thought is that people join informal economy and they shift to this parallel sector because it is a substitute option available for them and that also has some sort of benefits and hope for the negligence and disadvantaged group of society. Extra market regulations react to increase in the size of shadow economy. It is the expression of peoples' "needs" where state fails to satisfy. This school does not consider informal sector as a spinoff of pre-capitalist or current capitalist economic system (Gёrxhani, 2004; Chen, 2005; Chen et al., 2004; De Soto, 1989; Williams et al., 2006; Williams, 2006, 2007 and Contini, 1983). Therefore, existence of informal sector is the massage of excessive regulations. They are political powers that propagate a true picture of democracy and lucid circumstances of the market (Williams et al., 2006).

Taking into consideration informal sector while making economic policies will not only help true democracy to prevail in the country but also at the same time will reflect the true competitive market condition of the country. Schaefer (2002) comments that parallel to Dualist feeling, who are the proponents of no relationship between both sectors, certainly there is an association between shadow and official sectors. After including wage and nonwage work in informal sector, it can be deducted that both sectors have affiliation to each other. Like in the informal

50   Theories of Shadow Economy

sector some labor is present who works in both sectors while some merchants work for official firms on percentage or commission base.

Instead of looking from the perspective of formal and informal setting, the informal economy can be seen from a social perspective. Social capital, social connection, conviction, and institutions quality also play vital roles to explain informal sector. Today's globalized world has vanished the distance between formal and informal economies and put reservation of the distinction of formal and informal. In modern globalized world, there are many factors involved to link both sectors like social connection and network, friendship and kinship on the one hand and government social welfare policies on the other hand are reduced to substantial level the distinction between both economies, that is, formal and shadow (Sindzingre, 2006).

According to Portes (1994), social network's concept is more efficient and gives flexible hand to the state to grow and develop, while division of economy between official and unofficial reduces these benefits. Instead of using the notion of regulations, it is better to use the idea of social linkages because the concept of social connections provides new shape to the shadow economy, which is far beyond regulation impression.

Taking points from classical school of economics, the neoliberal school of thought considers overregulation as a source of reducing development and progress of private businesses. This is why they are joining informal sector to sustain and preserve their business. Shadow economy has been claimed to be fruitless since the quality of labor is low and they practice traditional business models, even though the advantages of official sector is open for all and everyone regardless working in formal or informal (Porta and Shleifer, 2008). However, in order to escape from government regulations (since it is too costly to be afforded by small businesses) they choose to function in shadow economy instead of formal economy. Thus, it is the government regulations that segregate formal from informal sector and thus we can say that economic activities that are out of the range of government regulations are called informal activities or shadow economies (Willman-Navarro, 2008).

In Legalist school, there are two opinions, that is, neoliberal, which expresses their view regarding a small promising postcolonial informal sector, and a group of scholars, that is, postcapitalist, whose concentration remains only in advanced countries while some of them look at the developing countries' shadow economy too (Williams et al., 2006). These postcolonial scholars are sharing land with neoliberals as they also consider shadow economy as an alternative to the official economy but divergent in the ground that people join and stay in informal sector not because of overregulation but because of the complex nature of formalization and the multifaceted working lifestyle in formal economy (Williams, 2005). They also accept the fact that shadow economy is the reality of social life and cannot be denied. In the words of Williams and Round (2008: p. 303), "we need to recognise, value and create informal practices that are already here and emerging so as to shine a light on the demonstrable construction of alternative possibilities".

Theories of Shadow Economy 51

Both neoliberal and postcolonial agree that shadow economy is alternative to official economy, but they disagree for the reason of joining shadow economy. Neoliberals propose that it is due to overregulation while postcolonials propose that it is due to the complex nature of work environment and complex ways of formalization. Neoliberal school of scholars criticize overregulation on the ground that overregulation not only stops the growth of private businesses but at the same time kills them to sustain, they are compelled and pushed toward shadow economy.

We can deduct from the arguments of neoliberal and postcolonial scholars that it is either overregulation or complexity in formalization that leads to increase shadow economy, which in reverse means that increase in shadow economy decreases in official economy.

To conclude, this school is inclined toward classical school of economics and suggests laissez-faire (no government intervention) in the market. They consider that shadow economy is created by the government itself because of intervention in economy in the form of too much regulation and business documentation requirements and formalities. It is the response of the deprived class of society to the failure of government to fulfill their economic needs and provide efficient services concerning businesses. It has become almost impossible for the micro, small, and medium enterprises to follow the complicated regulations and bureaucratic procedures of government. Therefore, in order to avoid such regulations and procedures, these firms transfer to shadow economy. So, the solution to the issue of shadow economy is not to make regulations for it because it is created by regulations in the first place.

To relate with our study, this proposition is not so obvious in the case of OIC economies, because the businesses in informal economy are very small and therefore remain unregistered because of their tininess. Therefore, they are mostly ignored by the government officials because of their small size. But on the other hand, there are some medium-level firms and business activities who want to register and benefit from official economy facilities and services but because of too much complexity in the documentation process they stay in unofficial sector.

So, because of low quality of institutions in OIC economies, there is always a way to bribery, kinship, connection, and favoritism, which somehow affects the decision of informal business to register and join official economy. Therefore, informal firms do stay informal and avoid being exploited by these corrupt government authorities. Based on this theory of the Legalist school, until and unless quality of institutions in OIC economies are improved and the confidence level of informal firms on government officials are not build, they will remain in shadow economy. In addition, shadow economy is the reflection of country political and market conditions, because bad government, weak form of democracy and undemocratic political structure of economies are not a good place for firms and businesses to operate officially as we obverse that OIC economies are facing both issues, that is, undemocratic political systems (most of GCC countries) and weak democracy in other OIC nations. Combining all these factors are reflected in the large size of shadow economy in OIC countries.

52 *Theories of Shadow Economy*

5.4 Complementary Theory

This theory proposes that formal and informal sectors are complementary to each other, they both have interconnection, and because of their interdependency, they decline and grow simultaneously (Williams, 2007 and Williams et al., 2006). With the name of "reinforcement thesis" Williams (2006, 2007) points out that both sectors of the economy are cooperative rather than challengers to each other. It is a fact that shadow and official economies have different topographies, but it does not indicate that both do not resemble each other (Potts, 2008). As stated by International Labor Organization (2002) "there is no defined dichotomy or split between the informal economy and the formal economy. That is, what happens in the informal economy will have impact on workers and employers in the formal economy and vice versa".

In the same study, ILO (2002) further comments that besides differences, there are similarities between shadow economy and formal economy. We need to look at their co-occurrence and try to find a way to benefit from it in terms of absorbing the neglect population of the society and receiving benefits from them in terms of economic development of an economy in general and reducing poverty, income inequality and attaining maximum income level in specific. According to Benería (1989), Castells and Portes (1989), and Peattie (1982), the players in the shadow economy are not only the negligible part of a population, rather big guns are also participating in shadow economy. Economic growth of a country is never looked at as the outcome of gap between shadow and official economies rather it is always observed that both sectors play their part in such growth (Williams et al., 2006).

Some scholars consider shadow economy and supplement "mixed economies of welfare" provision whenever they discuss public welfare provision concepts. On the other hand, other groups of scholars propose even beyond welfare provision and contemplate a substantial part of shadow economy in economy of a country (Williams, 2006, 2007 and Williams and Windebank, 2003). We can say that in complementary theory, whenever first group of scholars discuss shadow economy regarding welfare provision, they consider mixed economies of welfare and add new concept to the public and private debate, that is, civil society while the second group of scholars say that shadow economy is not limited to welfare provision, rather it has an active role in the economy.

This school propagates the need and importance of informal sector in terms of creating business environments and job opportunities as well as having means to satisfy necessities and wants of the people who are operating in this sector. Accordingly, economic policies should not only consider official economy but at the same time there is a need to look at the production and employment capacity of informal sector as well, because it plays an important role in overall and general development of a country. So, this school is giving importance to both sides of the coin: informal and formal (Williams, 2006, 2007). Thus, it is apparent that both sectors have interconnectivities and interdependencies from many aspects, especially in the time of crisis or recession in official sector (Becker, 2004). While basing on some studies, the case of developing nations is interesting where compared to official economy, growth rate of informal economy is more prominent (Blunch, Canagarajah and Raju, 2001 and Chen et al., 2004).

In summary, we can say that complementary theory is more inclined toward going hand in hand of informal sector with formal sector while informal sector is supportive and cooperative to official sector especially in time of difficulties and glitches. One group of scholars' stresses on the policy makers to look beyond the conventional preference of "public-private welfare" and discover the broader prospects of "civil welfare" while another group of researchers even appreciate the contribution of informal sector to official economy.

This theory considers formal and informal sector complementary and interdependence to each other. Any change in formal economy will be reflected in informal economy and vice versa. In order to cooperate with official economy, shadow economy also provides job and business opportunities to fulfill people's needs. On the one hand, informal sector is a protection and source of income for deprived people, while on the other hand it is helpful for the legal economy in case of recession. They propose to bring shadow economy in welfare debate in place of public private interest there should be civil interest and it is demanded to harmonize both to create synergy and benefit from each other. Legal economy provides economic resources and business opportunities, while informal sector provides training and experience to the workforces and then applies them in formal sector. Consequently, the whole economy will benefit and grow.

5.5 Voluntarist/Rational Exit Theory

Adam Smith, the eighteenth-century economist, is often viewed as the father of economics. He first presented the idea that in general the costs and benefits from enumerations to the employees in terms of money and nonmonetary must be equivalent (Willis and Rosen, 1979). Voluntarist school of thought proposes that taking into consideration comparative advantages and opportunities, firms, businesses and workers choose to function in shadow economy as compared to formal economy (Maloney, 2004). Firms are considered unfair competition in informal sector and therefore it is relatively easy for the firms who are operating in informal sector to compete with their counterparts in the informal sector compared to official sector. Therefore, they leave official sector for informal by taking rational assessment of comparatively less-competitive market (Chen, 2012). The equation can be reversed, that is, flow from informal to formal, if firms find easiness in taxation and registration. In order to reduce cost of production, sometimes firms evade taxes and government rules by keeping small portions of formal labors and the remaining from informal sector. Sometimes, when the quality of taxation and social security system is low, and firms and workers feel that there are no obvious benefits to them from social security contributions and the payroll tax system, in place of paying social security, the workers may agree with firms to receive more payment and avoid paying social security. In summary, we can say that there are some firms and workers who join informal sector after doing cost and

54 *Theories of Shadow Economy*

benefit analysis. The choice to join shadow economy is sometimes based on their personal choice, that is, voluntarily they join informal sector after looking to the relative advantages and sometime societies and cultures decide to choose a sector to join (Chen, 2012).

Assuming that advanced and developing nations small entrepreneurs share the same kind of characteristics. Previously, in developed nations, retirement planning and medical insurance have been covered by companies, while now they are not; therefore, they have not seen any security in formal sector and as a result join informal economy. In addition, if compensation of employees is elastic in formal market then decrease in wages in formal sector will compel workers to leave official economy for shadow economy because of getting more monetary wages. The process of diversion from formal to informal becomes even faster if the social security system fails to satisfy the desires of workers in terms of getting benefits compared to their payment or cost. This departure can further be fueled with insolvent labor market policy that restricts labor mobility in official market. If this is the condition of the labor market, it is more economical to join informal market compared to formal (Balan et al., 1973 and Maloney, 2004).

Informal market is a safe haven for unskilled laborers in terms of elastic labor times, providing entrepreneurial skills and place of job training on the one hand, while avoiding taxation and government market regulations on the other hand (Arias and Khamis, 2008). Therefore, the selection of informal sector is always based on relative advantages. There are two main things behind selection of profession. First, workers always choose professions that satisfy their desires and meets their talents. Additionally, workers also prefer a profession that yields a relatively better return (Lucas, 1978 and Rosen, 1982).

Based on economics' theory of maximization, individuals always look for maximization of utility while firms' maximization of return; if both individuals and firms realize that informal sector maximizes their utility and profit, respectively, both will join it voluntarily. Laborers with low talent and working experience are accepting low returns and prefer to stay in shadow economy in order to enjoy flexible job timing and no regulations, which are more economically plausible and utilitarian to them as compared to working and doing business under tough routine and inelastic government regulations. Similarly, in order to get maximum satisfaction and utility, the skillful and brilliant laborers as well as most experienced and talented individuals are remaining in formal economy as they have the ability to bear competition in the market and receive goods returns and better job packages (Arias and Khamis, 2008).

To summarize, according to this school, shadow economy players are choosy, and they select informal sector after doing costs and benefits analysis, which is based on their rational assessment of both sectors. Formal economy is facing many problems, like economic crises and failure of government, where government is only concerned about big firms while minor enterprises and entrepreneurs are ignored, therefore it is safe for them to operate in shadow economy. There are many advantages of formal economy like health insurance and social security, but people who are working in informal sector have no interest in these rewards because they prefer to have flexible labor hours and take-home salary even if it is less. In case of a bad social security system, more people will join shadow economy since they consider that the costs of social security are more as compared to the benefits. As a result, total revenue of government decreases as compared to government expenditure. This is what we observe in many OIC economies that are always facing budget deficits; even recently Saudi Arabia borrowed from IMF. In addition, in most of the developing economies, population is growing faster than economic growth, where the economy is not able to accommodate all labor force, therefore they are joining to shadow economy. In case of OIC economies, the majority of OIC countries are the developing nations and facing the same problem. Every year, substantial numbers of people join labor force while the economies are not able to provide jobs to all of them, which pushes many people toward shadow economy.

5.6 Illegalist Thought

Neoliberal and neoclassical schools of thought propagate this doctrine and consider that shadow economy is black, underground, or hidden economy and the reason behind joining it is to get advantages of shadow economy in terms of evading business rules, taxes, costs of power and energy, rents, and charges of doing business in official economy. The goods and services produced in this economy are illegal, underground, and black. Businessmen and laborers are intentionally operating in black market or even criminal activities to incentivize their business and labor, where there is no government taxes and regulations on one hand and trading black and illegal goods and services on the other hand (Maloney, 2004).

United Nations Economic Commission for Europe (1993) slightly differentiates underground and illegal production of goods and services. The underground production is a production of goods and services that are produced deliberately and are kept hidden and secret from the government officials, which are otherwise lawful and permissible if produced in the formal economy following rules and regulations of the state. While on the one hand, illegal production denotes the production of goods and services that are totally prohibited according to the constitution of the state or the production of goods and services termed as illegal because of the execution by the unlawful agents. But it should be noted that regardless of an illegally produced or underground entity, in both cases, on the one hand, government is losing taxes and other revenues which creates a hurdle in terms of government expenditure on public, while on the other hand, these activities violate state regulations, which makes it difficult for the government officials to impose law and order in the country.

The application of illegal or underground notions are not very convincing in low and developing economies. Because of feeble economic structure, on the one hand, and the social and economic issues like poverty and inequality on the other hand, survival and subsistence notions are more logical to apply in these economies. On the contrary, advanced and transitional countries are more suited to relate Illegalist theory because there is no convincing motto to operate in shadow

56   *Theories of Shadow Economy*

economy for survival because of low level of poverty (WIEGO, 2011 and Hussmanns, 2004). Because of illegal activities, there is a huge loss to the government in term of violation of laws, namely property rights, taxation, labor, enforcement of contracts, fees, and fines. Besides avoidance of regulations, illegal activities create hurdles to benefit from official economy, too. Similarly, informal sector's disadvantages are also for the informal sector's players themselves, like social security and financial sector services facilities of credit (WIEGO, 2011).

To close, this notion is proposed by neoclassical and neoliberal where they consider informal economy is hidden, underground, black, illegal, and even based on criminal activities. The goods and services produced in this economy are illegal and black where there are no regulations, taxes, costs of energy and power. The players of this sector get revenue by trading black and illegal goods and services. Similarly, their revenue also consists of criminal activities. Sometime the goods and service are legal but are executed by unlawful agents, which makes them illegal; this is called underground production. All these activities are totally prohibited by the law and constitution of the country.

This school separates illegal production from underground production where illegal production consists of criminal activities or black market which is illegalized by the constitution. While on the other hand underground production is not illegal by itself but it is executed by illegal and unlawful ways. In both cases, on one hand, government is losing revenue and as a result facing problems financing its expenditures, while on the other hand, these activities violate state regulations, which makes it difficult for the government officials to impose law and order in the country.

If we see this theory in the context of OIC member countries where most of these economies are facing the problem of illegality where government is losing a lot of revenue, that is why the government is always dependent on external sources like borrowing from capital market by issuing government securities like sukuk or loan. Therefore, we can say that shadow economy is one of the reasons to have less tax revenue, fees, registration charges, and so on, which in combined effect reduces total revenue of government while the expenditures/spending is more. As a result, government is facing a budget deficit due to less revenue because of shadow economy. In addition, it is one of the major hurdles to government in terms of imposing law and order in the country.

5.7 Inclusionist Perspective

The proposition of inclusionist is based on the idea that it is socioeconomic policies of government and the structure of governance that creates hurdles to small businesses and workers to get access to urban facilities like housing, places for jobs, and financing for doing business. They put more concentration on collective organisation and pro-poor urban planning (Meagher, 2013, 1995). Similarly, the postcolonial model, which is used in modern planning, does not consider shadow economy an exceptional from development policies, rather they give important place to shadow economy in urban developmental policies. Therefore, this act of

Theories of Shadow Economy 57

inclusion of shadow economy to the developmental policies is also appreciated by collective organisation and pro-poor urban planning (Roy, 2005).

Both schools of thought, that is, Pro-poor urban planning and collective organisation stress planned populations, unity of nations, and rearrangement of relationships. Thus, these elements define rules and regulations for the inclusion and exclusion of a deprived class of society to stay and get employment in the urban sector. But there are some worries regarding these poor males and females who are included in urban developmental policies because urban areas facilitating services, like property and home, are sometimes not enough, even though these are not expensive, while on the other hand, these urban facilities are sometimes even if they are sufficient. Therefore, sometimes it is better to remain exclusive (informal sector) for the poor as compare to join official sector because the terms and conditions are hostile and inequitable (Brown and McGranahan, 2016 and Du Toit and Hickey, 2007). Here terms and conditions mean to create an environment in the market where individuals evade exclusion and prefer to be included in civic society. So, urban planning and collective organisation are a great support to merge informal sector with official sector.

This school of thought is also in favor of green economy. Even though it is not directly mentioned in the contents, they are approaching the idea through financial inclusion. The collective organisation emphasizes urban planning authority to use their power and handle the issue of environment while on the other hand, pro-poor urban planning emphasizes that collective organisation should be supported with different sources, like creating competition between official and unregulated sectors (Mitlin and Satterthwaite, 2013 and Lindell, 2010).

In summary, inclusionist considers shadow economy heterogeneous and much diversified in nature, which is not open to the same government policies as in official economy. Similarly, if regulations are designed to green the official economy without taking into consideration unofficial sector, then it is difficult to achieve green economy. Finally, inclusive urban development and pro-poor urban planning both are suggesting negotiation and consultative approach to handle the issue of shadow economy. Economic and social policies, and structure of governance themselves create hurdles to small businesses and workers to get access to urban facilities like houses for living, places for jobs, and financing for doing business.

Collective organisation and pro-poor urban planning appreciate the act of inclusion of the postcolonial model, which uses modern planning where they consider shadow economy as an important part of urban developmental policies. Collective organisation and pro-poor urban planning are on the greater support of inclusion and claim that there are many other benefits of inclusion definitely to the poor class of society.

5.8 The Modern Perspective

The modern approach is more general; it covers shadow economy from all sides and considers all types of workers and businesses in the shadow economy. As we mentioned, there are controversies regarding the definition of shadow economy.

58 *Theories of Shadow Economy*

Therefore, the modern theoreticians give attention to offer a universal definition of shadow economy by using statistics, and improved measurement techniques. Similarly, some contemporary scholars have focused on the association between official economy and shadow economy, more specifically the impact of official economy regulations on informal sector, while some others have taken a look at the structure of shadow economy and tried to understand its mechanism (Chen, 2012).

Institutional economists look at shadow economy from the economic development perspective. They consider that shadow economy is a result of divergence and clash between two types of institutions, namely informal and formal, where from informal they mean household, social modes, cultural ethics, while on the other hand, regulations for economy and political and economic policies are considered formal. The advantages will appear, if the decision of formal institutions comply with expectation of informal institutions and vice versa.

The modern approach is a holistic approach and integrates all schools of thought. They suggest applying any of the aforementioned theories to the appropriate part of shadow economy. For instance, if there is overregulation and some businessmen and workers decide to join shadow economy, this comes under the scope of Legalist, while some others become part of informal economy by choice, which is the study area of voluntarist. On the other hand, there are certain entrepreneurs and laborers in shadow economy who work as a subsidiary for big companies and should be studied under structuralist; similarly dualist school can be used to study that part of shadow economy that consists of poor people who are involved in informal economic activities to earn their sustenance and have less ties with official sector.

According to modern approach shadow economy is heterogeneous and complex in nature, therefore it is very difficult to cover all its aspects by testing a single theory. The main question they ask is about the elements that provide foundation to shadow economy and they answer the question by dividing these elements into three main categories, that is firm, state, and individual. The modern theory accepts the reality that each aspect of shadow economy is important. For example, some individuals join it in order to survive, others enter because of tradition and custom; other than that many participate owing to regulations and costs of doing business in official economy. In addition, some others connect as a result of barrier to enter formal economy. All of the aforementioned are obstacles to many individuals and firms who are willing to be a part of official economy (Chen, 2012; Tokman, 2001 and Standing, 1999).

In the modern globalized world, the nature of world economies has changed drastically where the movement of factors of production among countries, boost in international trade, and decentralization of factors of production have played important parts in shadow economy. Before that, there would be contracts among firms in one economy, but now due to global economy, firms of different countries keep some official workers and with the support of modern communication, they hire the rest from other nations, which creates huge value to the firms in terms of avoiding pension funds, social security, and payroll expenses (Tokman,

Theories of Shadow Economy   59

2001). Challenging the marginalization proposition of Dualist school, they argue that shadow economy cannot be detached from today's global economy and current capitalist world, on the one hand, shadow economy nurtures entrepreneurs' business skills and on the other hand provides experience and training to young workforces (Hart, 2012; Neuwirth, 2011; Williams and Nadin, 2010 and Chen, 2005; Williams, 2008).

Finally, we can say that the modern approach looks at shadow economy holistically and suggests integration of all schools of thoughts. They consider shadow economy a heterogeneous and complex phenomenon; therefore, it is very difficult to cover all its aspects by testing a single theory. Generally, they look at shadow economy from all aspects and try to provide universal definition. Besides, institutional economists believe shadow economy is the result of a clash between formal institutions (rules, regulations, political and economic policies) and informal institutions (household, social modes, culture and ethics). If the decision of formal institutions is according to the expectation of informal institutions, shadow economy will decrease and vice versa.

Nowadays, many online projects are done by people from all over the world and there are many online businesses that use the services of different skilled laborers like IT specialists from other nations where there is no social security and pay roll taxes and other costs that the firms bear while having official workers. It is also a reality that shadow economy increases during economic downfalls and crisis (Tokman, 2001), and some people are forced to join shadow economy (ILO, 1972); others join because of culture and tradition (Chen, 2012).

5.9 Shadow Economy Theories Application to OIC Countries

From the preceding discussion, we can conclude that shadow economy is a complex, sophisticated, and heterogeneous phenomena and cannot be explained by a single theory. In this section, we are going to evaluate OIC economies in the context of the aforementioned theories. First, we cannot say that any specific theory suited to OIC economies, as we have discussed earlier that some theories fit into one aspect of shadow economy, while others fit into other segments. Second, as we have mentioned before, one of the objectives of this study is to find the determinants of shadow economy in OIC countries and then to compare them with non-OIC economies. Based on World Bank ranking, this study divided countries between low and high income, and we observe that most of the OIC member countries are low income and developing. Therefore, from a theoretical perspective, the distribution of OIC economies into two segments are not far away where informal economy can grow and cultivate its seeds.

We are evaluating each theory one by one in the context of OIC economies; first we see Dualist argument to be applied to OIC, where Dualist approach is the view that both shadow and official are totally isolated from each other. There is a place for Dualist theory, as there are a lot of deprived people who are living below the poverty line. Taking into consideration these parts of people in OIC economies, Dualist view can be applied. Second, the structuralists consider

60 *Theories of Shadow Economy*

shadow economy a secondary and subordinate part of official economy. If we look at the Structuralists view, there are both big firms and small enterprises in OIC economies. Normally on average it is difficult to support this proposition that these small unregistered firms are created by big firms who provide first step production materials to firms given that there is government authority who keeps an eye on these big firms' production processes, supply chain, and so on, as they are registered and part of official economy and benefiting from the facilities of formal economy, that is, financing and capital market. But this proposition can be supported from the angle of the black market. As we see from the World Governance Indicator ranking that the majority of OIC economies fail to have good institutions.

If the institutional quality is low, there is always a way to corruption and black market. So, these big firms can subordinate small firms in shadow economy that becomes supportive for supply chain. Third, the proposition of Legalist is that overregulation causes shadow economy. The proposition of Legalist does have applicability in OIC countries because small businesses that are operating in the informal economy are producing at a small level and do not need registration because of their small size. Therefore, they are ignored by the government officials. On the other hand, there are some medium-level firms that want to register and benefit from official economy facilities, but because of too much complexity in the documentation process they stay in unofficial sector. Fourth, complementary theory proposes that formal and informal sectors are complementary to each other. If we see this theory in the context of OIC, there are a lot of workers who gain experience, skills, and training in informal sector and then join formal sector is obvious in many OIC economies. Fifth, according to Voluntarist, business enterprises and entrepreneurs choose informal sector, after doing costs and benefits analysis, which is based on their rational assessment of both sectors in OIC countries. We observe that low quality of institutions, political instability, burdensome taxation, and finally social security are the main factors that make formal sector costly and informal sector beneficial to operate.

Sixth, Illegalists who consider informal economy hidden, underground, black, illegal, and even consist of criminal activities. Looking at OIC economies from an Illegalist perspective, we know that most of the OIC members' countries are developing nations, while in most of the developing economies population is growing faster than their economic growth and the supply of labor force becomes more in relation to working opportunities. As a result, some of the labor force joins illegal, black, and even criminal activities in order to survive. These illegal activities create hurdles to law and order in the country. In addition, because of these black and illegal markets, OIC economies are losing a lot of revenue, in one way they are facing budget deficits due to less revenue, while on the other hand they are always dependent on external sources like borrowing thorough capital by issuing government securities like Sukuk or bonds.

Seventh, Inclusionists ruminate that economic and social policies and structure of governance exclude small businesses and workers to get access to urban facilities like houses for living, places for jobs, and financing for doing business. We

Theories of Shadow Economy 61

find that on average the size of shadow economy in OIC countries is 34.6% of GDP. The entrepreneurs and enterprises that are operating in informal sector are restricted to facilitate legal economy credit and financing servicing. Because they do not have collateral and other requirements. Here Islamic finance can come in and play a role through Islamic micro financial institutions (IMFI) or Islamic social businesses to grow these entrepreneurs and enterprises and merge them into official economy. In addition, the government of OIC economies should include shadow economy in their developmental policies as suggested by pro-poor urban planning. Another problem with OIC economies is the urbanization. In recent decades a lot of urbanization has taken place, which has populated big cities and has created huge increases in property prices. But OIC economies fail to accommodate these flows of people and develop their cities according to the modern urban development planning. There are many reasons for urban migration but one of the obvious reasons is looking for job opportunities. The problem becomes even worse when these people cannot find a job and are excluded from financial facilities. Here again Islamic finance can play a role to provide interest-free loans and Islamic micro finance facilities to these people in order to start businesses and maintain their sustenance, which comes under the inclusive urban development planning notion of Inclusionist.

Eighth, according to the modern approach, shadow economy is heterogeneous and complex in nature, therefore it is very difficult to cover all its aspects by applying a single theory. Of course, this notion is more realistic and holistic and covers all segments of informal economy while applying to OIC member countries. As discussed before, all of the aforementioned theories have some application in OIC economies but to a segment of shadow economy. For example, Dualists are mostly concerned about deprived and poor segments of shadow economy, while Illegalist's approach is mostly concerned about black markets. Application of Dualist theory is that most of OIC countries are low-income countries. So, Dualist approach can be used to study this segment of shadow economy in OIC economies. While in OIC countries, there are a lot of black markets and illegal activities that can be studied by applying the proposition of Illegalist. But if we want to study the overall shadow economy then the modern approach should be used, as it covers all aspects of shadow economy.

To summarize, in this section theories of shadow economy have been examined as we go from the origin of shadow economy up to modern times. The Dualist school regards shadow economy separated or with a limited link with official economy. Structuralist school says that formal and informal economies are interrelated and connected to each other while small firms and labor in shadow economy are subordinate to the official economy in big firms. While Legalist school considers that shadow economy is the response and reaction to the overregulation and complications in business documentation by the state. Opposite to this is voluntarists who hold the position by saying that the people themselves choose informal sector by making rational decision after doing cost-benefit analysis of both sectors. Complementary theory highlights that both formal and informal economies are cooperative rather than substitute to each other. Both can co-occur,

62   *Theories of Shadow Economy*

grow, and decline simultaneously. Similarly, informal sector can help official sector especially in the time of difficulties and glitches. As far as the Illegalist theory is concerned, advanced and transitional countries are more suited to relate Illegalist theory with them. This school is more inclined toward illegal activities where people are operating in black markets and even criminal activities are followed to incentivize their businesses by trading black and illegal goods and services.

The common thing in all theories is their application to certain segments of shadow economy and their limitation to apply other parts of shadow economy. So, each school of thought should be studied in its own domain and cannot cover all segments of shadow economy. After analysis of the aforementioned theories, observe that some people are in shadow economy by compulsion, others are joining it by choice, some others seek survival, and quite a number of people are there because of culture and tradition. After evaluation, it is also found that the nature of shadow economy is heterogeneous, complex. It is also realized that shadow economy increases at the time of economic downfall and crisis.

Finally, the modern perspective, which is also called realist theory, accepts that all the aforementioned theories have more or less practicality and application to explain shadow economy in a given domain (ILO/WTO, 2009 and Chen, 2012). But modern view combines all the previous theories, in order to capture all aspects of shadow economy and get deeper understanding of overall phenomenon. There are three basic factors: firm, state, and individual, which provide foundation to shadow economy, and in addition, it is the undetectable part of the modern globalized world.

6 The Model and Empirical Investigation of Shadow Economy

This chapter consists of three sections. In section 6.1, the estimating models are presented. Section 6.2 covers the method of estimations, while section 6.3 contains sources of data and descriptions of the variables. Additionally, the first section has three subsections: estimation equations for the determinants of shadow economy, estimation equations for financial development impact on shadow economy, and estimation equations for financial inclusion impact on shadow economy. Similarly, section 6.3 has one subsection, that is, variable. Finally, the chapter has a conclusion.

6.1 The Estimating Models

This section explains the equations used to achieve the objectives of this study. Each equation is explained in connection to its corresponding objective.

6.1.1 Estimation Equations for the Determinants of Shadow Economy

In line with Schneider and Enste (2000), we develop the following equations to investigate empirically the determinants of shadow economy in OIC economies and then compare it with non-OIC countries. The following equations have been specified:

First, we use full sample and then we split the data into OIC and non-OIC countries subsamples in order to address the following equations.

$$
\begin{aligned}
LSE_{it} = \alpha_0 &+ \alpha_1 LSE_{it-1} + \alpha_2 LECOF_{it} + \alpha_3 LTF_{it} + \alpha_4 LT_{it} + \alpha_5 LGDP_{it} \\
&+ \alpha_6 LGE_{it} + \alpha_7 LMS_{it} + \alpha_8 LPS_{it} + \alpha_9 LRQ_{it} + \alpha_{10} LBF_{it} \\
&+ \alpha_{11} LROL_{it} + \alpha_{12} D1_{it} + u_{it}
\end{aligned}
\tag{6.1}
$$

In equation 6.1, u is error term, i shows countries, while t denotes time period. The dependent variable LSE shows shadow economy, which is in percentage of GDP and comes from Medina and Schneider (2017). LSE_{it-1} is the lag of dependent variables, that is, shadow economy; this lag of dependent variable is included in the model to consider for the possible dynamic nature of shadow economy. Following Schneider et al. (2010), we include economic freedom ($LECOF$) variable

DOI: 10.4324/9781003329954-6

64　*The Model and Empirical Investigation of Shadow Economy*

as a proxy to capture the market easiness. This proxy is used to see how the market has a business-friendly environment in order to attract businesses and entrepreneurs from shadow economy to official sector.

Economic freedom ($LECOF$) is in percentile, ranging from 1 to 100, the higher the better. Studies like Schneider et al. (2011), Onnis and Tirelli (2011), and Berdiev et al. (2018) investigated the association between trade freedom and business freedom with shadow economy, therefore, we include trade freedom (LTF) and business freedom (LBF), which are in percentile in order to capture how much that market has a trade friendliness and a business friendliness environment. In line with Remeikiene and Gaspareniene's (2015) prediction that international trade plays an important role in shadow economy, we also considered international trade (LT) (% of GDP) to account for import and export relevance with shadow economy. Similarly, gross domestic product ($LGDP$), which is an annual percentage growth rate, is also included in the model because of its close association with shadow economy. Studies like Schneider (2011), Hassan and Schneider (2016), Lucinda and Arvate (2005), and Schneider and Hametner (2014) among others found evidence for gross domestic product association with shadow economy. Likewise, government expenditure (LGE) is also considered one of the important determining factors of shadow economy. As said by Dell'Anno et al. (2018), Mahmoudzadeh et al. (2017), and Beck and Hoseini (2014), government expenditure increases the size of shadow economy and has connection with shadow economy.

One of the determinants of shadow economy is money supply (LMS),[1] which is also considered by Hassan and Schneider (2016) and Elgin and Uras (2013), taking into consideration the Legalist school of thought view that overregulation causes shadow economy. Similarly, in empirical literature, significant association has been found between shadow economy and institutions (Abdih and Medina, 2013; Dreher et al., 2009 and Schneider, 2010). We include regulatory quality (LRQ), rule of law ($LROL$), and political stability (LPS) to control of institutions effect. All three variables, that is, political stability (LPS), regulatory quality (LRQ), and rule of law ($LROL$), are in percentile. We use dummy ($D1$) to differentiate OIC countries from non-OIC countries. If the country belongs to OIC group, we assign 1, otherwise 0. Except dummy ($D1$) variable, all other variables are in the natural logarithm form. We transformed the variables into the log forms in order to control for variation, linearize a relationship, and help us in an interpretation.

In order to find the determinants of shadow economy in OIC and non-OIC countries, we divide the full sample into two subsamples, that is, OIC and non-OIC countries, and we have estimated the following equations.

$$LSE_{it} = \alpha_0 + \alpha_1 LSE_{it-1} + \alpha_2 LECOF_{it} + \alpha_3 LTF_{it} + \alpha_4 LT_{it} + \alpha_5 LMS_{it}$$
$$+ \alpha_6 LGDP_{it} + \alpha_7 LGE_{it} + \alpha_8 LRQ_{it} + u_{it} \tag{6.2}$$

Equation 6.2 represents the dependent variable LSE, that is, shadow economy. t denotes time period, u is error term, and i shows countries. We also consider lag of dependent variable, LSE_{it-1}, in order to control for possible passed year effect on today shadow economy. In order to represent market easiness, we also

The Model and Empirical Investigation of Shadow Economy 65

consider economic freedom (*LECOF*), which is in percentile rank and ranges from 1 to 100 (Schneider et al., 2010). The trade freedom (*LTF*) is also counted in so as to look after possible association between shadow economy and trade freedom (Onnis and Tirelli, 2011; Schneider et al., 2011 and Berdiev et al., 2018). In the same way, taking into consideration the close association between formal and informal economy, gross domestic product (*LGDP*) is also brought into the equation. In the literature, many studies found significant evidence for both variables' association (Lucinda and Arvate, 2005; Schneider and Hametner, 2014; Schneider et al., 2011 and Hassan and Schneider, 2016). As per the association of shadow economy and government expenditure (*LGE*) is concerned, we find studies such as Dell'Anno et al. (2018), Mahmoudzadeh et al. (2017), and Beck and Hoseini (2014) who investigated the association between government expenditure and shadow economy and found positive association between both independent variable (government expenditure) and dependent variable (shadow economy). Finally, no one can ignore the role of institutions with respect to shadow economy (Schneider, 2010; Abdih and Medina, 2013 and Dreher et al., 2009). We use political stability (LPS), regulatory quality (LRQ)[2] and rule of law (LROL) proxies for institutions. Variables are transformed into natural log form to get coefficients in elasticities forms.

6.1.2 Estimation Equations for Financial Development Impact on Shadow Economy

Following Capasso and Jappelli (2013), Bayar and Aytemiz (2017), and Maki (2012) we present the following models to investigate empirically the impact of financial development on shadow economy in both groups of nations. The following equation has been specified:

$$LSE_{it} = \beta_0 + \beta_1 LSE_{it-1} + \beta_2 LFD_{it} + \beta_3 Controls_{it} + \beta_4 D1_{it} + \epsilon_{it} \tag{6.3}$$

We include in equation 6.3, LSE_{it} (shadow economy) as a dependent variable, where t denotes time period, u is error term, and i captures countries. The past year effect on today shadow economy has been controlled by count in the lag dependent variable, LSE_{it-1}. To test the impact of financial development on shadow economy, we have used domestic credit to private sector (% of GDP) as a proxy for financial development (*LFD*). It is the best proxy to represent financial development of an economy. In the literature, many studies use it, like Bayar and Ozturk (2016), Din et al. (2016), and Bayar and Aytemiz (2017). $D1$ is a dummy variable. We assign 1 if the country belongs to OIC members and 0 if it is not so. The coefficient of β_4 tells us the difference between OIC and non-OIC countries. Based on the previous papers, like Berdiev and Saunoris (2016) and Capasso and Jappelli (2013), we expect β_2 (the effect of financial development on shadow economy) to be negative. Similarly, in control variables, we included unemployment (*LU*) (% of total labor force) because of its strong association with shadow economy, when it comes to relationship between both variables. In the literature,

66   *The Model and Empirical Investigation of Shadow Economy*

we found studies like Hassan and Schneider (2016), Dell'Anno et al. (2004), and Schneider et al. (2010) who found significant association between unemployment and shadow economy.

Due to close association between trade and shadow economy, international trade (LT) is also included in the equation to control for possible effect on shadow economy following Remeikiene and Gaspareniene (2015). Correspondingly, in line with Schneider (2011), Hassan and Schneider (2016), Lucinda and Arvate (2005), and Schneider and Hametner (2014) that gross domestic product has association with shadow economy, we include gross domestic product ($LGDP$), which is an annual percentage growth rate. Equally, according to Dell'Anno et al. (2018), Mahmoudzadeh et al. (2017), and Beck and Hoseini (2014), government expenditure has positive impact on shadow economy and is one of the significant factors of shadow economy, therefore, we also consider it, that is, government expenditure (LGE). In order to control for regulations aspects, we take in political stability (LPS) and regulatory quality (LRQ). Abdih and Medina (2013), Dreher et al. (2009), and Schneider (2010) found that institutions matter for shadow economy size. The variables that are used to achieve the second objectives are also in the natural logarithm forms, except dummy variable ($D1$).

To see the impact of financial development on shadow economy specifically in OIC countries, the OIC dummy has been interacted with financial development in order to differentiate financial development impact on shadow economy between OIC and non-OIC countries. Thus, the following equation is specified:

$$LSE_{it} = \beta_0 + \beta_1 LSE_{it-1} + \beta_2 LFD_{it} + \beta_3 D1_{it} + \beta_4 Controls_{it}$$
$$+ \beta_5 (D1_{it} * LFD_{it}) + \epsilon_{it} \tag{6.4}$$

Here we count in equation 6.4, the dependent variable, which is shadow economy, LSE_{it}. On the other hand, to take care of possible dynamic nature of shadow economy the lag of the dependent variable (LSE_{it-1}) is also counted inside the equation. u is error term, i shows countries, while t denotes time period. The association between shadow economy and financial development has been tested by using domestic credit to private sector (% of GDP) proxy to capture financial development (LFD) following Bayar and Ozturk (2016), Din et al. (2016), and Bayar and Aytemiz (2017).

As we are also interesting to see the impact of financial development on shadow economy in OIC countries compared to non-OIC countries, dummy ($D1$) has been interacted with financial development in order to see if there is any difference in its impact on shadow economy with respect to OIC countries verses non-OIC countries. Here in equation 6.4, ($D1*LFD$) is the interactive term of OIC dummy with financial development. The interpretation of the interaction term β_5 in equation 6.4 depends on the coefficient of β_5. If the main effect β_2 (financial development (LFD)) is positive and the coefficient of β_5 ($D1*LFD$) is also positive, it would mean that the positive effect is stronger for the OIC countries. Similarly, if the main effect β_2 (financial development (LFD)) is positive and the coefficient of β_5 ($D1*LFD$) is negative, it would show that the effect is weaker in case of

The Model and Empirical Investigation of Shadow Economy   67

OIC countries. Furthermore, if the main effect β_2 (financial development (LFD)) is negative and the coefficient of β_5 ($D1*LFD$) is also negative, it would depict that the negative effect is stronger for the OIC countries. $D1$ is a dummy variable. We assign 1 if the country belongs to OIC members and 0 if it is not so. The coefficient of β_4 will tell us the difference between OIC and non-OIC countries. In line with literature, we expect β_2 to be negative (Capasso and Jappelli, 2013 and Berdiev and Saunoris, 2016). As per the control variables are concerned, we consider unemployment because shadow economy and unemployment have a strong relationship with shadow economy (Hassan and Schneider, 2016, Dell'Anno et al., 2004, and Schneider et al., 2010). According to Remeikiene and Gaspareniene (2015) the linkage between shadow economy and trade is significant. Therefore, international trade (LT) is also included in the model.

6.1.3 Estimation Equations for Financial Inclusion Impact on Shadow Economy

To examine empirically the impact of financial inclusion on shadow economy in both types of countries, the following equation has been stated following Singh et al. (2012), Din et al. (2016), and Bittencourt et al. (2014).

$$LSE_{it} = \beta_0 + \beta_1 LSE_{it-1} + \beta_2 LFI_{it} + \beta_3 Controls_{it} + \epsilon_{it} \tag{6.5}$$

Equation 6.5 consists of shadow economy index (LSE_{it}) while LSE_{t-1} is the lag dependent variable of shadow economy. We have used four proxies' variables to represent financial inclusion (LFI) along with control variables. Among these four variables are automated teller machines (ATMs) per 100,000 adults denoted by ($LATM$), bank deposits to GDP (%) symbolized by (LBD), bank branches per 100,000 adults, which is signified by (LBB), and bank credit to bank deposits (%), which is represented by ($LBCBD$). t means time period, i captures countries, while ε_{it} implies disturbance term. The coefficient of β_2 denotes the impact of financial inclusion on shadow economy in case of full sample. If the sign of β_2 is positive, then we conclude positive impact of financial inclusion on shadow economy, and in case of negative sign, we predict inverse relationship between both variables, given that it is statistically significant. As far as control variables are concerned, we considered money supply (LMS), which is an annual percentage growth of broad money following Hassan and Schneider (2016) and Elgin and Uras (2013). In line with Schneider et al. (2011) we also counted in GDP per capita ($LGDPP$) which is an annual percentage growth. Another important variable is tax ($LTAX$), which is measured of total tax as a percentage of GDP. The expansion and the size of shadow economy will be more if the gap between after-tax revenue and cost of labor in formal economy are high (Schneider, 2005). To capture market constrains, we added monetary freedom (LMF), which is in percentile, ranging from 1 to 100, the higher the better, consistent with Ouédraogo (2017) and Schneider et al. (2010) that market constrains are one of the important causal factors of shadow economy. According to Ela (2013), unemployment boosts shadow economy,

68   The Model and Empirical Investigation of Shadow Economy

therefore we counted in total unemployment (LU), which is a percentage of total labor force.

We further interact dummy ($D1$) with financial inclusion proxies to see the impact of financial inclusion on shadow economy in OIC countries. Hence, we develop the following specification:

$$LSE_{it} = \beta_0 + \beta_1 LSE_{it-1} + \beta_2 LFI_{it} + \beta_3 D1_{it} + \beta_4 Controls_{it}$$
$$+ \beta_5 (LFI_{it} * D1_{it}) + \epsilon_{it} \qquad (6.6)$$

Equation 6.6 includes shadow economy (LSE_{it}), in order to control for dynamic nature of shadow economy; the lag dependent variable (LSE_{it-1}) of shadow economy is also counted in in the equation. We have used four proxies' variables to represent financial inclusion (LFI) along with control variables. t means time period, i captures countries, while ε_{it} implies disturbance term. LFI signifies financial inclusion, which consists of four proxies: bank branches (LBB) per 100,000 adults, bank credit to bank deposits (%) ($LBCBD$), automated teller machines ($LATMs$) per 100,000 adults, and bank deposits to GDP (%) (LBD). The coefficient of β_2 is the expression of association. If the sign of β_2 is positive, then we conclude positive relationship between financial inclusion and shadow economy, and if the coefficient has negative sign, we predict inverse relationship between financial inclusion and shadow economy, as long as it is statistically significant. To specify equation accurately, following the literature, many control variables are included in the model, that is, money supply (LMS), GDP per capita ($LGDPP$), tax ($LTAX$), monetary freedom (LMF), unemployment (LU), and international trade (LT) (Hassan and Schneider, 2016; Elgin and Uras, 2013; Schneider et al., 2011; Schneider, 2005; Ouédraogo, 2017; Ela, 2013 and Remeikiene and Gaspareniene, 2015).

We add two more variables where $D1$ denotes dummy variable and takes the value 1 if the country belongs to OIC member nations and 0 otherwise. Second, we interact $D1$ dummy with financial inclusion ($LFI_{it}*D1$) to see whether the impact of financial inclusion in case of OIC member nations is different or not. The resulting coefficient of β_5 tells us the financial inclusion impact on shadow economy given that the country is from OIC nations. If the β_2 is positive and the β_5 is also positive, it would mean that the positive effect of financial inclusion is stronger for the OIC countries. Similarly, if the β_2 is positive and the β_5 is negative, it would show that the effect of financial inclusion is weaker in case of OIC countries. Furthermore, if the β_2 is negative and the β_5 is also negative, it would represent that the negative effect of financial inclusion is stronger in OIC countries.

6.2 The Method of Estimations

Taking into consideration the preceding equations, we use panel data. There are many benefits of panel data compared to cross-section data and time series (Baltagi et al., 2005). For instance, panel data estimation techniques relax the assumption

The Model and Empirical Investigation of Shadow Economy   69

of homogeneity and consider that countries are heterogeneous in nature. Therefore, countries heterogeneity is controlled. On the other hand, cross-section and time series data do not take into account heterogeneity and, hence, are open to bias estimates. Second, panel data implies efficient estimators, more degree of freedom, and variability, while identification and measurement of different effects can be easily detected by using panel data as compared to using only time series or cross-sectional data. Finally, cross-sectional data observing steady and escape a multitude of variations, while usage of panel data remains to be well-matched in terms of understanding dynamics of adjustment and taking into consideration duration of economic conditions.

Taking into consideration the advantages of panel data, dynamics of countries and the nature of our variables, especially shadow economy index, we use dynamic panel system GMM technique.

As our numbers of countries (141), that is, N is more than time period (7), that is, T. Second, according to O'Conner (1983) prior to industrialization, shadow economy existed and remained the means of livelihood in pre-capitalist civilizations, which shows the persistent nature of dependent variable. Likewise, the majority of OIC member countries are developing and shadow economy remains persistent in developing countries too, and at the same time has a long memory in developed countries too (O'Conner, 1983). So, based on the dynamic and long memory nature of our dependent variable, we estimate all equations by applying GMM method. Normally, economic variables associations are dynamic in nature, especially shadow economy where passed year shadow economy may affect today shadow economy. In order to comprehend such dynamic tuning, panel techniques are best suited for estimation. The persistent nature of shadow economy can be captured with dynamic techniques, too.

According to Baltagi et al. (2005), if there exists legged dependent variable along with independent variables, then a dynamic relationship will exist. So, the relationship between dependent variable and independent variables along with lagged dependent variable are given here:

$$SE_{it} = \theta SE_{i,t-1} + \beta x'_{it} + \mu_{it} \qquad i = 1, \ldots, N; t = 1, \ldots, T \qquad (6.7)$$

In equation 6.7, θ is a scalar, where β is K × 1 while x'_{it} is 1 × K. Similarly, μ_{it} based on the econometrics assumption of straight error component form:

$$u_{it} = \mu_i + v_{it} \qquad (6.8)$$

In equation 6.8, μ_{it} is an error term, which is identically distributed, while μ_i captures individual heterogeneity, that is, individual specific effect, whereas the remaining disturbance is denoted by v_{it}. Equation 6.8 is persistence over time for two reasons, that is, heterogeneity and autocorrelation. So, heterogeneity is checked by individual effects, while autocorrelation is taken out by lagged dependent variable ($SE_{i,t-1}$), which exists among explanatory variables. Furthermore, SE_{it} is a function of μ_i as well as $SE_{i,t-1}$. As a result, autocorrelation also exists

70 The Model and Empirical Investigation of Shadow Economy

between μ_i and $SE_{i,t-1}$, that is, lagged dependent variable (shadow economy). So, the model consists of autocorrelation between μ_i and $SE_{i,t-1}$. Therefore, we cannot apply pooled ordinary least square method because the estimator we get by using pooled ordinary least square will be inconsistent and biased, given that serial correlation does not exist for v_{it} (Baltagi, 2008). Similarly, the effect of such correlation goes further to the dynamic panel model where it makes the estimator biased for traditional panel models like fixed effect (FE). Thus, in that case, we cannot apply it. Additionally, in our case $N > T$ because we have 141 countries (N) and seven years (T) and 11 years (T). But if $T \rightarrow \infty$ then the estimator that we get by using fixed effect (FE) of θ and β becomes consistent in traditional dynamic model. Equally true for random effect (RF) estimator to be biased in dynamic penal model owing to the restriction of execution quasi-demeaning. However, in case of application of random effect to our models, there will be correlation between $(SE_{i,t-1} - \Theta\,SE_{i,-1})$ and $(\mu_{it} - \Theta\,\mu_i, -1)$. To conclude, due to autocorrelation, traditional panel techniques, that is, fixed effect (FE), random effect (RE), as well as pooled OLS estimators turn to be biased.

Conversely, Anderson and Hsiao (1981) proposed instrument variables model, to take out the individual effects, μ_i, by taking simply first difference of the model and then using just $SE_{i,t-2}$ or extended $\Delta SE_{i,t-2} = (SE_{i,t-2} - SE_{i,t-3})$ as an instrument for $\Delta SEi,t - 1 = (SEi,t - 1 - SEi,t - 2)$. Similarly, in this case there will be no correlation between instruments and $\Delta v_{it} = (vit - vi,t - 1)$ provided that there is no serial correlation in vit themselves. So, the problem of endogeneity, which we mentioned before, can be addressed by using estimation method, which is based on instrumental variables technique. However, it should be noted that instrumental variables-based method would only work if there are appropriate instruments for endogenous independent regressor. In order to satisfy the validity of instruments, there are two main conditions: non-collinearity and relevancy. Non-collinearity means that the newly created instrumental variable should not be correlated with vit (disturbance terms), while relevancy means that the newly created instrumental variable must have high correlation with endogenous regressor for which this instrument is created. However, because of not utilizing all the available movement conditions, even though the estimator based on instrumental variable has consistency but may not be efficient estimates of the parameters. Second, if the correlation of instrumental variable with the respective endogenous variable is weak, then the instrument loses its relevancy and effectiveness. Finally, the instrumental variable also does not take into consideration error terms (vit) different pattern (Ahn and Schmidt, 1995).

As opposed to Anderson and Hsiao (1981), generalized method of moments (GMM) technique has been advised by Arellano and Bond (1991), which, in relation to instrumental variable technique, is more efficient. According to them, one can attain additional instruments if orthogonality conditions has been used, which stands between disturbance terms (vit) and lagged values of Y it. They further suggest that in order to make movement conditions, first difference of powerfully exogenous covariates can be utilized. First difference can be utilized to remove

The Model and Empirical Investigation of Shadow Economy   71

individual effects and to obtain consistent coefficient of θ, where T is fixed and $N \rightarrow \infty$. For example, $t = 7$ or $t = 11$ and the association is given as $SE_{i7} - SE_{i6} = \theta (SE_{i6} - SE_{i5}) + (vi7 - vi6)$, in this case, the instrumental variable SE_{i5} is effective, in this case having strong correlation with $(SE_{i6} - SE_{i5})$ and no correlation with $(vi7 - vi6)$, given that there is no serial correlation in vit themselves. Similarly, increasing valid instrumental variable along with succeeding period, for T, valid instrumental variable (IV) becomes $(SE_{i1}, SE_{i2}, SE_{i3}, SE_{i4}, \ldots \ldots SE_i, T - 2)$. The movement conditions are said to be GMM-type movement conditions if it is developed in such a way where specific legged levels of the dependent variable are independent (orthogonal) toward Δvit (differenced disturbances). The movement conditions will be standard instrumental variable movement conditions if it is designed by using strictly exogenous covariates. Arellano and Bond (1991) offered two step GMM estimator by utilizing these movement conditions. They based their first step on the assumption that error terms are homoscedastic as well as independent throughout the countries and years. While in the next step, consistent estimate of the variance-covariance matrix can be achieved by using the error terms estimated in the first step. So, now the assumptions of homoscedastic as well as independent can be relaxed, and the estimator grounded on the preceding conditions is called GMM difference estimator. But in difference GMM, weaknesses have been identified by Blundell and Bond (1998) while applying to the labor demand model utilizing company panel data. They found that the GMM estimators have poor finite sample properties. Which shows that the estimator is not anymore unbiased in a condition where the correlation between the first differences and their corresponding legged level of the series are weak. So, this weak relation indicates that instrumental variables, which are utilized for the first differenced of the equations, are poor. In addition, they demonstrate that the problem will be increased in case of marginal process become exceedingly persistent. Thus, the AR (1) model has been specified as follows:

$$SE_{it} = \delta SE_{i,t-1} + \eta_i + \upsilon_{it} \tag{6.9}$$

In equation 6.9, it is assumed that υ_{it} is serially uncorrelated with themselves. According to Blundell and Bond (1998), there are two situations in which the instrumental variables that are utilized in the standard first-differenced GMM estimator lose their information. The first situation is where autoregressive parameter δ consist of unit root, that is, δ approaches to 1, while the second situation is where the η_i upsurges as compared to the υit. The same issue (finite sample properties in AR (1) of GMM estimator) has been examined by Blundell and Bond (1998) in their Monte Carlo study. They find weak performance of first-differenced estimator because of rise in the values of δ. So as to handle these weaknesses in the difference GMM estimator, Blundell and Bond (1998) and Arellano and Bover (1995) suggest extra stationarity restriction on the original conditions process, which allows us to apply system GMM estimator, which takes advantage of lagged differences of SE_{it} as instrumental variable for equations in level forms

72 The Model and Empirical Investigation of Shadow Economy

other than lagged levels of SE_{it} as instrumental variables for first differences form equations.

Therefore, system GMM estimator has been considered to be efficient in relation with traditional first difference GMM estimator particularly when (autoregressive) AR parameter, that is, δ tends to unity, while η_i rises in relation to υ_{it}. These levels restrictions become useful as first difference instruments term into poor (Blundell and Bond, 1998). Lastly, in the presence of variables that are close to random walk, system GMM estimator is considered to be better and more suitable in relation to the difference GMM, on the condition that difference GMM estimator experiences poor instrumental variables problem (Sarafidis et al., 2009; Bond and Windmeijer, 2002 and Roodman, 2009). Besides the aforementioned issue with difference GMM, according to Roodman (2009), one more issue with difference GMM technique is that it intensifies the gaps and distances if the data is unbalanced panels. Therefore, we get inspiration to use forward orthogonal deviations transformation, which is recommended by Arellano and Bover (1995).

As per the objective of this study, we need to isolate OIC countries from non-OIC in order to know whether OIC countries are different from non-OIC countries or not. Based on the aforementioned advantages of system GMM over difference GMM and considering our main interest in OIC dummy (where OIC dummy become omitted because of differencing in difference GMM). We choose to use system GMM technique as our method in our study.

Roodman (2009) set a rule of thumb; if the coefficient of lagged dependent variable at minimum is 0.8 then it shows that there is a high level of persistency in the series. In such a situation, based on simulation, the system GMM results will be most convincing. According to Windmeijer (2005), by raising the coefficient of the lagged dependent variable for the two-step system GMM at a minimum of 50% compared to the two-step differenced GMM estimator. It would be a signal that system GMM estimator becomes capable to correct the downward biasedness of difference GMM estimator by utilizing a more convenient set of instruments. However, system GMM is also not free from issues, like too many instruments can be effective from an individual perspective but jointly can over-fit the endogenous variables and therefore in case of finite samples might remain invalid. At the same time, too many instruments weaken Hansen test of overidentification (instruments joint validity test) (Roodman, 2009).

To summarize, our data consist of large N, that is, 141 countries and small-time series ($T < N$). Therefore, we use system GMM in our study as our main statistical technique. According to Bond et al. (2001), GMM technique takes care of endogeneity, temporary measurement errors, and omitted variable bias. In case of omitted variable bias, like countries located in the same geographical location might be associated with explanatory variables. As the characteristics of one country differ from another, thus, if not controlled for time-invariant fixed characteristics, their influence can be accumulated in error terms and as a result, can make the estimator biased if not included into the model. This issue can be addressed by taking first difference and then the estimates achieved by GMM will be free from such problem of biasness. Similarly, in order to handle the issue of

The Model and Empirical Investigation of Shadow Economy 73

nonconsistency, GMM utilizes lagged variables as instruments and through these instruments exogenous part can be extracted from independent variables to ensure consistency of the parameters. Correspondingly, Bond et al. (2001) suggest that in case of existence of temporary measurement errors, utilizing lagged levels of independent variables for variables in differences as instruments will make the parameters potentially consistent. After getting the result by using system GMM, we need to see the required tests. GMM need only two tests, one is overidentification and the other is autocorrelation. For autocorrelation, we need to look at Arellano and Bond (1991) test of no autocorrelation in the first-differenced errors.

On the other hand, for instruments overidentification restriction, Sargan (1975) test is used. To test Arellano and Bond (1991) autocorrelation we have H0, which shows that there is no first order AR (1) serial correlation and therefore H0 must be rejected while the absence of second order AR (2) serial correlation of the first-differenced errors must be upheld. Because we need disturbance term to have identical distribution and remain independent as it is important for the GMM estimates to be consistent. Inversely, for Sargan test, H0 shows that overidentifying restrictions are valid, which indicates these instruments are valid only if they have no correlation with the errors in the first-differenced equations.

As mentioned before, we use two-step system GMM technique as well as Windmeijer (2005) correction in order to reduce two-step standard errors downward biasness. Taking into consideration too many instruments issue, we follow Roodman's (2009) rule of thumb. He proposed to collapse the instrument matrix if the instruments are more than the group. Especially in our case, even though our countries are 141 and data spanning is annual and small ($N > T$). But still it is sometimes needed to collapse the instruments, especially if they are more than numbers of groups. Therefore, we collapse instruments where needed. In addition, choosing system GMM in our case is due to the fact that we are using OIC dummy in our estimation where difference GMM cannot work. Specification of robust standard errors give us variance-covariance estimates that are robust in the case of heteroscedasticity. When we specify Windmeijer corrected (wc-robust) standard errors, the distribution of Sargan test becomes unknown. In such a situation, Hansen test can be used to test overidentifying restrictions. We are using Roodman (2006, 2009) second generation Xtabond2 command, which gives us Hansen test statistic, which is the minimum value of two-step GMM criterion function. Where for Hansen test the null hypothesis (H0) is that overidentifying restrictions are valid. We evaluate the robustness of our estimation by many ways like changing the proxy variable, counting additional variable, and so on.

6.3 Sources of Data and Description of the Variables

In this study, the number of countries under consideration are 141, where 42 belong to OIC member nations and the remaining 99 are non-OIC countries. We have used two data sets and collected from five different sources: Word Development Indicator (WDI), World Governance Indictor (WGI), International Monetary Fund (IMF), World Heritage Foundation (WHF), and United Nation Government

74　*The Model and Empirical Investigation of Shadow Economy*

Revenue Dataset 2017. To estimate the determinants of shadow economy, we used the data spanning from 1995 to 2015 after taking an average of every three years. Thus, we got average seven years, that is, combined each three years into on, which is in line with Law and Singh (2014). There are two advantages of taking an average; first, it covers the missing values and second, it reduces the number of observations from 21 to 7, which is best suited for the technique (GMM) applied in this study. Similarly, the selection of data set is based on the availability of data and variables of interest. To explore the impact of financial development and financial inclusion on shadow economy, we utilized data spanning from 2004 to 2015. This period of data set is selected because data related to financial inclusion variables are available from 2004 onward. To normalize, we have transformed the data into natural logarithm form.

6.3.1 Variables

The dependent variable, that is, shadow economy (LSE) data came from the Medina and Schneider (2017) study, which covers 158 countries over the 1991 to 2015 period. They estimated the index of shadow economy by using multiple indicators and multiple causes (MIMIC) model, which are considered to be the best method to estimate the size of shadow economy compared to currency demand, electricity consumption, and other methods. We use economic freedom (LECOF) variable as a proxy to capture the market easiness. This proxy is used to see how the market has a business-friendly environment in order to attract all kind of businesses from shadow economy toward official sector. Schneider et al. (2010) also used economic freedom variable to apprehend market easiness. Economic freedom (LECOF) is in percentile, ranging from 1 to 100, the higher the better. Gross domestic product (LGDP), which is an annual percentage growth rate, has close connection with shadow economy. Some studies like Schneider (2011) and Hassan and Schneider (2016) revealed that shadow economy decreases with an increase in GDP growth rate. Others, like Lucinda and Arvate (2005) and Schneider and Hametner (2014), found evidence for both variables' association.

Government expenditure (LGE) (% of GDP) plays an important role in the decision of joining shadow economy, as increase in government spending compels businesses to leave formal sector as they are not able to compete in the market. According to Dell'Anno et al. (2018), government expenditure leads to add more people into the shadow economy, as it distorts economic resources. Mahmoudzadeh et al. (2017) and Beck and Hoseini (2014) also found connection between government expenditure and shadow economy. Another important variable is money supply (LMS) (annual percentage growth rate), which is used by Hassan and Schneider (2016) and Elgin and Uras (2013). Unemployment (LU) is measured of unemployment as a percentage of total labor force. According to Ela (2013), due to lack of skill and education, workers who are migrated to urban areas from rural areas are not able to get employment in the official sector. Therefore, for sustenance they join shadow economy. Tax (LTAX) is measured of total tax as a percentage of GDP. The expansion and size of shadow economy will be more in case of higher taxation (Schneider, 2005). To capture the impact of import

The Model and Empirical Investigation of Shadow Economy   75

and export on shadow economy, international trade (LT) (% of GDP) is used as a control variable. Firms compel to shift to shadow economy, if imports are more than exports, because it may affect domestic firms', that is, small and medium enterprises to compete with foreign firms (Remeikiene and Gaspareniene, 2015). In order to capture the role of institutions in shadow economy, political stability (LPS), regulatory quality (LRQ), and rule of law (LROL) are utilized as proxies to indicate quality of institutions. All three variables are in percentile, the nearer to 100, the better. The role of institutions in shadow economy has been given much importance, both in empirical and theoretical literature. Similarly, institutions quality is considered one of the main determining factors in explaining shadow economy (Dreher et al., 2009; Schneider, 2010 and Abdih and Medina, 2013). Except dummy variable, all other variables are in the natural logarithm form.

To test the impact of financial development and financial inclusion on shadow economy, we have again used shadow economy as a dependent variable and utilized domestic credit to private sector (LDC) (% of GDP) as a proxy for financial development. Domestic credit to private sector is used to represent financial development in the literature (Bayar and Ozturk, 2016; Din et al., 2016 and Bayar and Aytemiz, 2017). Similarly, we included unemployment (LU) (% of total labor force) because of its strong association with shadow economy, when it comes to relationship between both variables (Hassan and Schneider, 2016; Dell'Anno et al., 2004 and Schneider et al., 2010). The variables that are used to achieve the second objectives are also in the natural logarithm form except dummy variable. Finally, to analyse the impact of financial inclusion on shadow economy, we have used four proxies' variables to represent financial inclusion along with control variables. Among these four variables are Automated Teller Machines per 100,000 adults denoted by (LATM), bank deposits to GDP (%) symbolized by (LBD), bank branches per 100,000 adults, which is signified by (LBB), and bank credit to bank deposits (%), which is represented by (LBCBD).

As we are interesting in addressing the shadow economy through financial inclusion in OIC countries and then compared with non-OIC countries, our main variables include bank credit to bank deposits (%), which is represented by (LBCBD), bank deposits to GDP (%), symbolized by (LBD), automated teller machines per 100,000 adults, denoted by (LATM), and bank branches per 100,000 adults, which is signified by (LBB).

We have selected these four variables because of their importance in the contest of OIC economies and to cover long enough time spans. Even though the World Bank provides many proxies for financial inclusion, data are available for only 2011 and 2014. One of the best tools to deal with shadow economy is the availability and accessibility of the formal financial facilities for all members of the society. The financial exclusion and thus shadow economy can be reduced, if a majority of the people have access to formal financial services. The automated teller machines per 100,000 adults represents the ownership of accounts. We presume that the ownership of accounts shows the people and businesses accounts with formal financial institutions. Even though the best way to measure financial inclusion is to count the number of people and firms who have accounts, but the

76 The Model and Empirical Investigation of Shadow Economy

World Bank data are limited to 2011. The automated teller machines per 100,000 adults denoted by (LATM) are used to represent the ownership of accounts, because generally an automated teller machine card is tied with an account when someone has an account with a formal financial institution. We have used bank branches per 100,000 adults (LBB) as a measure to capture penetration rate of financial institutions. Because with the help of bank branches number we can deduce prevalence of financial institutions in the countries. Bank credit to bank deposits (LBCBD) is used as a proxy to measure the conversion of deposit into the credit. Bank deposits to GDP (%) symbolized by (LBD) is utilized to capture the constrains to have account with banks. While studying financial inclusion and economic growth in OIC countries, Kim et al. (2018) used these proxies to measure financial inclusion. Similarly, the importance of access to finance has been pointed by Cumming et al. (2014) and Neaime and Gaysset (2017), while studying financial inclusion in MENA countries.

6.4 Conclusion

To summarize, this section discusses determinants of shadow economy the impact of financial development on shadow economy in OIC and non-OIC countries. Similarly, it also finds out the effect of financial inclusion on shadow economy in both types of countries. The study has used panel data, which is extracted from five different sources: WDI, WGI, WHF, IMF and UNGR. We considered 141 countries in which 42 were OIC member states while the remaining 99 were non-OIC economies. The study has used system GMM technique.

Notes

1 Money supply is the sum of currency outside the banking system that is the time, savings, demand deposits, foreign currency deposits with banks and traveler's checks.
2 We report regulation quality (LRQ) in main results Table 7.3 while political stability (LPS) and rule of law (LROL) results are reported in appendices Tables A1 and A2.

7 Results and Discussion

In the previous chapter we discussed sources of data, explained variables, developed estimated equations, and elaborated on a method used in this study. In the current chapter, we present descriptive statistics and correlation analysis. Furthermore, the chapter also presents detailed analyses and estimations. This chapter is divided into four sections. Section 7.1 discusses the results of the determinants of shadow economy. The impact of financial development on shadow economy results are discussed in section 7.2. Section 7.3 highlights the results of association between shadow economy and financial inclusion. In section 7.4 the robustness tests are reported, followed by the concluding remarks.

7.1 Descriptive Statistics

Before proceeding to the estimation of the determinants of shadow economy and the impact of financial development and financial inclusion on shadow economy, we present the descriptive statistic in Table 7.1. The mean value of shadow economy (LSE) is 1.43 and has a standard deviation of 0.19, whereas the mean value of LGDP is 1.69 and has a standard deviation of 0.07. The maximum value of shadow economy (LSE) is 1.83 and the minimum is 0.90. The average of government expenditure (LGE) is 1.16, while standard deviation is 0.15 showing low variation. The mean value of economic freedom (LECOF) is 1.78 and has a standard deviation of 0.07, the mean value of political stability (LPS) is 1.53 and standard deviation is 0.39. The mean value of regulation quality (LRQ) is 1.63 and standard deviation is 0.32. The average value of rule of law (LROL) is 1.57 and standard deviation is 0.39. Institutional variables, that is, political stability (LPS), regulation quality (LRQ), and rule of law (LROL) have relatively low averages compared to economic freedom. As far as financial inclusion is concerned, the mean value of ATMs per 100,000 (LATM) is 1.32 and standard deviation is 0.68, whereas the average of bank deposits as a percentage to gross domestic product (LDB) is 1.56 and standard deviation is 0.35. On the other hand, the mean value of domestic credit to private sector as a percentage of gross domestic product (LDCPS) is 1.56 and standard deviation is 0.43. All three variables, that is, ATMs per 100,000 (LATM), bank deposits as a percentage to gross domestic product (LDB), and domestic credit to private sector as a percentage of gross domestic product (LDCPS) have low variation. Similarly, the mean value

DOI: 10.4324/9781003329954-7

78   Results and Discussion

of bank branches per 100,000 adult (LBB) is 1.01, which is relatively low, while standard deviation is 0.51.

Table 7.1 displays summary statistics of variables used in this study. Shadow economy (LSE) is measured as shadow economy as a percentage of gross domestic product. Gross domestic product (LGDP) is measured as an annual percentage change in gross domestic product. Money supply (LMS) is measured as money supply as an annual percentage change in money supply. Government expenditure (LGE) is measured as the final consumption expenditures of general government as a percentage of gross domestic product. Tax (LTAX) is measured of total tax as a percentage of gross domestic product. Trade (LT) is measured as the total trade as a percentage of gross domestic product.

Unemployment (LU) is measured of unemployment as a percentage of total labor force. Political stability (LPS) measures perceptions of the likelihood of political instability as in percentile rank. Regulation quality (LRQ) captures perceptions of the ability of the government to formulate and implement sound policies and regulations that permit and promote private sector development as in

Table 7.1 Descriptive statistics

Variable	Obs.	Mean	Std. dev.	Min.	Max.
LSE	1,691	1.435522	0.195728	0.90091	1.839352
LGDP	1,690	1.609084	0.071585	−0.52281	1.875054
LMS	1,444	1.840636	0.107714	−0.50190	3.495978
LGE	1,677	1.161641	0.156815	0.31114	1.499316
LGDPP	1,690	1.592492	0.076558	−0.76929	1.845287
LTAX	1,599	−0.84745	0.254562	−2.41199	−0.31331
LT	1,689	1.905021	0.213799	1.324783	2.646031
LU	1,680	0.816986	0.317503	−1	1.575188
LPS	1,692	1.536955	0.38974	−0.32428	2
LRQ	1,692	1.632385	0.326653	−0.30963	2
LROL	1,692	1.571171	0.394141	−0.32838	2
LECOF	1,682	1.781229	0.073881	1.330414	1.954725
LBF	1,682	1.801511	0.115088	1.369216	2
LAMT	1,472	1.327461	0.685285	−1.92176	2.460344
LBD	1,628	1.567518	0.354213	0.346353	2.680943
LBB	1,611	1.010011	0.510770	−0.92082	2.411114
LBCBD	1,630	1.953401	0.21499	1.250176	2.944315
LDCPS	1,644	1.560791	0.436893	−0.72125	2.494363
LMF	1,682	1.866381	0.146256	0	1.974512
LTF	1682	1.858340	0.103880	0	1.977724
LINF	1,675	1.617122	0.115013	−0.78695	4.388226
LVA	1,692	1.588919	0.346215	0.27368	2

(LSE) is shadow economy. All the other variables include (LGDP) gross domestic product, money supply (LMS), government expenditure (LGE), GDP per capita (LGDPP), trade (LT), tax (LTAX), unemployment (LU), (LPS) political stability, (LRQ) regulation quality, (LROL) rule of law, (LECOF) economic freedom, (LBF) business freedom, (LATM) automated teller machines per 100,000 adults, (LBD) bank deposits to GDP, (LBB) bank branches per 100,000 adults, (LBCBD) bank credit to bank deposits, (LDCPS) domestic credit to private sector, monetary freedom (LMF), (LTF) trade freedom, inflation (LINF), and voice and accountability (LVA). For detailed descriptions, see section 6.3.1 and the variables summary Table A9 in Appendices.

percentile rank. Rule of law (LROL) captures perceptions of the extent to which agents have confidence in and abide by the rules of society, and in particular the quality of contract enforcement, property rights, the police, and the courts, as well as the likelihood of crime and violence, which is in percentile rank. Economic freedom (LECOF) measured economic freedom, which is the fundamental right of every human to control his or her own labor and property, is in percentile rank. Business freedom (LBF) measures the extent to which the regulatory and infrastructure environments constrain the efficient operation of businesses.

Automated teller machines (LATM) are the number of automated teller machines (per 100,000 adults). Bank deposits (LBD) is a measure of bank deposits as a percentage of gross domestic product. Bank branch (LBB) is the bank branches, which is the number of commercial bank branches (per 100,000 adults). Bank credit to bank deposits (%) (LBCBD) is a measure of private credit by deposit money of banks. Domestic credit to private sector (LDCPS) is the domestic credit to private sector, measured as domestic credit to the private sector by banks as a percentage of gross domestic product.

7.2 Correlation Analysis

In Table 7.2, we present the correlation among variables. The variables used in this study consist of causal variables, financial development proxy, and financial inclusion variables. The correlation signs of financial development and financial inclusion variables are consistent as the coefficients are high in magnitude ($r > 0.50$), while looking at correlation coefficients between determinants of shadow economy where institutional variables have high magnitude ($r > 0.40$) and consistent signs while other determinants have small magnitude. For example, the relationship of regulation quality (LRQ), rule of law (LROL), and political stability (LPS) with shadow economy (LSE) is negative. Some variables are highly correlated with others. So, as to avoid the potential statistical issue, we develop many equations.

7.3 Results and Discussion

In this section, the results of the determinants of shadow economy, financial development, and financial inclusion are presented by using different econometric models. We have divided the data into full sample and subsamples, that is, OIC and non-OIC countries in Table 7.3.

Similarly, we are interacting OIC dummy with financial development and financial inclusion variables. The interaction would reveal the differences, if any, between the OIC and the non-OIC countries, which are reported in Tables 7.5, 7.6, 7.7, and 7.8, respectively.

7.4 Determinants of Shadow Economy With Full Sample and Subsamples[1]

Table 7.3 provides results and discussion, that is, determinants of shadow economy. The selection of variables is based on theoretical and empirical

Table 7.2 Correlation coefficients of variables

	LSE	LGDP	LMS	LGE	LGDPP	LT	LTAX	LU	LPS	LRQ	LROL	LECOF	LBF	LATM	LBD	LBB	LBCBD	LDCPS	LMF	LTF	LINF	LVA
LSE	1																					
LGDP	0.03	1																				
LMS	0.12	0.21	1																			
LGE	−0.26	−0.13	−0.15	1																		
LGDPP	−0.01	0.97	0.18	−0.08	1																	
LT	−0.19	0.05	−0.01	0.11	0.06	1																
LTAX	−0.05	−0.03	−0.08	0.35	0.06	0.20	1															
LU	0.02	−0.09	−0.03	0.24	−0.05	−0.01	0.20	1														
LPS	−0.44	−0.01	−0.09	0.39	0.06	0.38	0.32	0.05	1													
LRQ	−0.50	−0.05	−0.17	0.42	0.02	0.22	0.26	0.09	0.57	1												
LROL	−0.56	−0.01	−0.15	0.47	0.06	0.21	0.24	0.09	0.65	0.89	1											
LECOF	−0.55	−0.08	−0.18	0.31	−0.02	0.28	0.18	0.04	0.52	0.87	0.79	1										
LBF	−0.50	−0.10	−0.16	0.39	−0.01	0.22	0.22	0.13	0.45	0.70	0.70	0.77	1									
LATM	−0.49	−0.14	−0.25	0.46	−0.03	0.19	0.26	0.14	0.55	0.63	0.63	0.57	0.65	1								
LBD	−0.55	−0.16	−0.27	0.35	−0.08	0.31	0.24	0.04	0.40	0.62	0.63	0.59	0.57	0.68	1							
LBB	−0.51	−0.09	−0.15	0.41	0.01	0.21	0.27	0.20	0.48	0.59	0.60	0.54	0.63	0.80	0.72	1						
LBCBD	−0.27	−0.07	−0.04	0.26	0.01	0.03	0.14	−0.07	0.28	0.35	0.33	0.28	0.32	0.38	0.04	0.33	1					
LDCPS	−0.61	−0.16	−0.25	0.39	−0.06	0.26	0.25	0.05	0.45	0.70	0.69	0.65	0.63	0.74	0.84	0.75	0.49	1				
LMF	−0.23	0.00	0.01	0.12	0.01	0.05	0.07	0.03	0.17	0.48	0.44	0.50	0.25	0.15	0.27	0.12	0.14	0.26	1			
LTF	−0.30	−0.09	−0.07	0.34	−0.03	0.21	0.19	0.04	0.31	0.46	0.37	0.48	0.37	0.43	0.30	0.37	0.21	0.35	0.16	1		
LINF	0.17	0.01	−0.01	−0.18	−0.01	−0.04	−0.08	−0.02	−0.19	−0.33	−0.32	−0.28	−0.16	−0.13	−0.19	−0.14	−0.10	−0.20	−0.49	−0.11	1	
LVA	−0.33	−0.09	−0.16	0.41	0.01	0.08	0.38	0.15	0.51	0.72	0.69	0.63	0.51	0.54	0.56	0.57	0.13	0.56	0.29	0.33	−0.22	1

The variables include (LSE) shadow economy, (LGDP) gross domestic product, money supply (LMS), government expenditure (LGE), GDP per capita (LGDPP), trade (LT), tax (LTAX), unemployment (LU), (LPS) political stability, (LRQ) regulation quality, (LROL) rule of law, (LECOF) economic freedom, (LBF) business freedom, (LATM) automated teller machines per 100,000 adults, (LBD) bank deposits to GDP, (LBB) bank branches per 100,000 adults, (LBCBD) bank credit to bank deposits, (LDCPS) domestic credit to private sector, monetary freedom (LMF), (LTF) trade freedom, inflation (LINF), and voice and accountability (LVA). For detailed descriptions, see section 6.3.1 and the variables summary Table A9 in Appendices.

Table 7.3 Determinants of shadow economy with full sample and subsamples

Dependent variable SE	Full sample			Subsample OIC			Subsample non-OIC		
	(1)	(2)	(3)	(1)	(2)	(3)	(1)	(2)	(3)
	FE	RF	GMM	FE	RE	GMM	FE	RE	GMM
L.LSE			0.8836***			0.8194***			0.4872***
			[0.096]			[0.089]			[0.049]
LECOF	0.0958*	0.0929*	−0.0605*	0.1080*	0.1060	−0.0031	0.1051	0.1029	0.0209
	[0.035]	[0.034]	[0.030]	[0.029]	[0.028]	[0.030]	[0.074]	[0.072]	[0.026]
LTF	−0.0906***	−0.0879***	0.0499**	−0.0954***	−0.0933***	−0.0061	−0.1089	−0.1077	−0.0416*
	[0.033]	[0.032]	[0.024]	[0.027]	[0.026]	[0.026]	[0.073]	[0.071]	[0.023]
LT	−0.1358***	−0.1303***	−0.0957**	−0.1213***	−0.1158***	−0.0911***	−0.1457***	−0.1337***	−0.1251***
	[0.028]	[0.027]	[0.042]	[0.039]	[0.037]	[0.031]	[0.039]	[0.036]	[0.020]
LGDP	**−0.0001****	**0.0001****	**−0.0025****	**−0.0007****	**−0.0007****	**−0.0039*****	**0.0004****	**0.0003**	**−0.0018*****
	[0.000]	[0.000]	[0.001]	[0.001]	[0.001]	[0.001]	[0.000]	[0.000]	[0.000]
LGE	**0.1539*****	**0.1413*****	**0.0710*****	**0.0826****	**0.0852****	**0.0667*****	**0.2381*****	**0.2240*****	**−0.0481**
	[0.033]	[0.031]	[0.022]	[0.035]	[0.034]	[0.023]	[0.048]	[0.047]	[0.036]
LMS	0.0280**	0.0295**	−0.0449**	0.0056	0.0059	0.0022	0.0415***	0.0435***	0.0301*
	[0.014]	[0.014]	[0.019]	[0.020]	[0.020]	[0.014]	[0.013]	[0.013]	[0.015]
LRQ	**−0.1076*****	**−0.1117*****	**−0.1240*****	**−0.0919*****	**−0.0930*****	**−0.0726*****	**−0.1086*****	**−0.1126*****	**−0.1359*****
	[0.009]	[0.009]	[0.042]	[0.013]	[0.012]	[0.017]	[0.014]	[0.014]	[0.016]
Constant	1.6525***	1.6619***	0.5678**	1.8208***	1.8087***	0.5431***	1.4837***	1.4853***	1.2497***
	[0.057]	[0.057]	[0.235]	[0.073]	[0.069]	[0.165]	[0.069]	[0.077]	[0.115]
Observations	975	975	838	424	424	365	551	551	473
Adjusted R-squared	0.463			0.4			0.534		
Instruments			14			43			24
Overall	141	141	141	62	62	62	79	79	79
Arellano-Bond: AR(1)			0.00			0.00			0.00
Arellano-Bond: AR(2)			0.9467			0.4601			0.4682
Hansen Test (p-Val)			0.6262			0.0729			0.0011
F-Stats (P-Val)			0.00			0.00			0.00

The dependent variable is shadow economy (LSE). L.LSE is the lag of shadow economy. All the other variables include (LECOF) economic freedom, (LTF) trade freedom, trade (T), (LGDP) gross domestic product, government expenditure (LGE), money supply (LMS), (LRQ) regulation quality. For detailed descriptions, refer to section 6.3.1 and the variables summary table A9 in Appendices. Standard errors are in parentheses and * p < 0.1, ** p < 0.05, *** p < 0.01 denote significance at 10%, 5%, and 1% respectively.

82 Results and Discussion

Table 7.4 Financial development and shadow economy with OIC dummy (D1)

Dependent variable SE	(1)	(2)
L.LSE	0.6748***	0.6749***
	[0.060]	[0.060]
LU	0.0676***	0.0677***
	[0.019]	[0.019]
LT	−0.1263***	−0.1255***
	[0.026]	[0.026]
LGDP	−0.0021***	−0.0021***
	[0.001]	[0.001]
LGE	0.1301***	0.1304***
	[0.032]	[0.032]
LPS	−0.0209*	−0.0204*
	[0.011]	[0.010]
LRQ	−0.0775***	−0.0778***
	[0.018]	[0.018]
D1		0.0037
		[0.017]
Constant	0.6791***	0.6755***
	[0.115]	[0.113]
Observations	838	838
instruments	36	37
overall	141	141
Arellano-Bond: AR(1)	0.00	0.00
Arellano-Bond: AR(2)	0.1489	0.1506
Sargan Test (p-Val)	0.0959	0.0901

The dependent variable is shadow economy (LSE). L.LSE is the lag of shadow economy. All the other variables include (LU) unemployment, (LT) trade, (LGDP) gross domestic product, government expenditure (LGE), (LPS) political stability, (LRQ) regulation quality, and (D1) dummy variable. For detailed descriptions, refer to section 6.3.1 and the variables summary Table A9 in Appendices. Standard errors are in parentheses and * $p < 0.1$, ** $p < 0.05$, *** $p < 0.01$ denote significance at 10%, 5%, and 1%, respectively.

literature (Chen et al., 2004; De Soto, 1989; Schneider et al., 2010; Schneider, 2011; Ott, 1998; Dell'Anno et al., 2018; Hassan and Schneider, 2016; Eilat and Zinnes, 2000; Dell'Anno, 2003; Ihrig and Moe, 2004; Schneider and Enste, 2000; Dell'Anno and Schneider, 2003; Dell'Anno, 2003; Ihrig and Moe, 2004; Razmi et al., 2013; Elbahnasawy et al., 2016; Torgler and Schneider, 2007; Dreher et al., 2009 and Abdih and Medina, 2013). The choice of dynamic model is justified as the lag coefficients in all models are significant. Diagnostic tests of autocorrelation, based on AR (1) and AR (2), are passed while overidentification restrictions are also satisfied, which are verified by Hansen test.

There are three main factors that need to be considered regarding shadow economy. The first one is macroeconomic fundamentals, such as gross domestic products (LGDP) and government expenditure (LGE). The second factor is freedom to do business in the official economy, for example, trade freedom (LTF), monetary freedom (LMF), and economic freedom (LECOF). The third factor is the role of

Results and Discussion   83

institutions in the shadow economy, which is measured by rule of law (LROL), regulation quality (LRQ), and political stability (LPS). In Table 7.3, we report results of the determinants of shadow economy. In the case of control variables, the coefficient of economic freedom (LECOF), in model (1), suggests that there is a negative impact of economic freedom on shadow economy, which is consistent with Dreher et al. (2009) and Abdih and Medina (2013). On the other hand, the coefficient of international trade (LT) is negative and statistically significant, which indicates that more international trade means less shadow economy. This is understandable as increase in international trade leads to more business and employment opportunities in official sector. These results are in line with Schneider et al. (2010). The coefficient of trade freedom (LTF) is positively significant, which expresses that trade freedom increases shadow economy, which is in contrast with Onnis and Tirelli (2011). One of the possible justifications can be that easiness in import licenses and regulations creates problems to the local firms to compete with foreign products, especially, if the foreign products are cheap. Consequently, they switch to shadow economy in order to reduce the cost of production, face less regulations and taxation, as well as benefit from informal sector's cheap labor. Therefore, trade freedom pushes businesses and entrepreneurs to shadow economy.

7.4.1 The Effects of Economic Growth on Shadow Economy

Table 7.3 represents the subsamples results along with the full sample. Besides GMM, we also present random effect and fixed effect results. In all the models' specifications, we see that the coefficient of gross domestic product (LGDP) remains negative and statistically significant across all models' specification except subsample of non-OIC (random effect) model (2), indicating that economic growth is negatively related to shadow economy. This finding predicts the relationship between economic growth and the shadow economy. The small coefficient of gross domestic product (LGDP) is an indication of the small impact of economic growth on shadow economy. Even though this finding is consistent with prior studies (Eilat and Zinnes, 2000; Dell'Anno, 2003; Ihrig and Moe, 2004; Schneider and Enste, 2000; Dell'Anno and Schneider, 2003 and Schneider, 2011) but the small coefficient of GDP can be justified that both sectors official and shadow economy are isolated from each other, which is in line with Dualist school (Hart, 1973; ILO, 1972 and Rothenberg et al., 2016).

7.4.2 The Effects of Government Expenditure on Shadow Economy

Similarly, Table 7.3 also suggests that government expenditure is positively related to shadow economy as the coefficient on government expenditure (LGE) is positive and statistically significant at 1% level in the majority of the models, suggesting that an increase in the government expenditure will lead to an increase in shadow economy. This finding predicts the positive relationship between government expenditure and shadow economy. These findings are consistent with several prior studies. For example, according to Dell'Anno et al. (2018), government

84   *Results and Discussion*

spending boosts shadow economy as it distorts in allocation of resources. Because sometimes, private firms fail to compete with public firms, especially if the private firms are small in size. As a result, spending by the government crowds them out from official sector and throw them into the shadow economy. Similarly, Hassan and Schneider (2016) and Schneider et al. (2010) have found that government expenditure increases shadow economy.

7.4.3 The Effects of Institutional Quality on Shadow Economy[2]

Continuing our investigation regarding the determinants of shadow economy, Table 7.3 shows the subsample results along with the full sample. Besides GMM we also present random effect and fixed effect results where the dependent variable is shadow economy (LSE). This result predicts the relationship between institutional quality and the shadow economy. This result is consistent with previous studies (Razmi et al., 2013; Schneider et al., 2010 and Schneider, 2010). Generally, the subsamples results are in line with the full sample results.

7.5 Financial Development and Shadow Economy

In Table 7.4, the choice of dynamic model is confirmed, as the lag coefficient in all models are significant. Diagnostic tests of autocorrelation, which are tested by AR (1) and AR (2) and overidentification restrictions tests are passed.

In model (1) in Table 7.4, the coefficient of unemployment (LU) is positively significant and hence reveals that unemployment increases shadow economy, which is in line with the existing literature (Nchor et al.,2016; Nchor and Adamec, 2015 and Dell'Anno et al., 2004).

The impact of international trade (LT) is also negatively significant, which shows that increase in international trade leads to decrease in shadow economy. This result is in line with Remeikiene and Gaspareniene (2015), who find that export reduces while import increases shadow economy. Predictably, gross domestic product (LGDP) growth reduces shadow economy. This is in line with Berdiev and Saunoris (2016), Giles and Tedds (2002) and Schneider et al. (2003). On the other hand, government expenditure (LGE) increases shadow economy. It is expected that increases in government consumption expenditure in the official economy instigates crowding-out effect and distorts competition in the market. Therefore, such increase in government consumption expenditure encourages individuals and firms towards shadow economy. The same results are found by Hassan and Schneider (2016) and Schneider et al. (2010). Similarly, institutional variables reduce shadow economy, which is in line with Schneider et al. (2010), Elbahnasawy et al. (2016), and Torgler and Schneider (2007).

7.5.1 The Effect of Financial Development on Shadow Economy

In this section, we present our empirical results regarding the effect of financial development on shadow economy. In Table 7.5 the dependent variable is shadow

Results and Discussion 85

Table 7.5 Financial development interaction with OIC dummy (D1)

Dependent variable SE	(1)	(2)	(3)	(4)
L.LSE	0.6748***	0.6749***	0.7739***	0.7815***
	[0.060]	[0.060]	[0.043]	[0.041]
LU	0.0676***	0.0677***	0.0330**	0.0350***
	[0.019]	[0.019]	[0.013]	[0.013]
LT	−0.1263***	−0.1255***	−0.0650***	−0.0663***
	[0.026]	[0.026]	[0.021]	[0.021]
LGDP	−0.0021***	−0.0021***	−0.0026***	−0.0026***
	[0.001]	[0.001]	[0.001]	[0.001]
LGE	0.1301***	0.1304***	0.0774***	0.0842***
	[0.032]	[0.032]	[0.021]	[0.020]
LPS	−0.0209*	−0.0204*	−0.0229**	−0.0222**
	[0.011]	[0.010]	[0.009]	[0.009]
LRQ	−0.0775***	−0.0778***	−0.0589***	−0.0613***
	[0.018]	[0.018]	[0.014]	[0.015]
D1		0.0037	0.0013	−0.0239
		[0.017]	[0.012]	[0.016]
LDC			**−0.0227***	**−0.0264****
			[0.012]	**[0.012]**
LDC_D1				**0.0172****
				[0.009]
Constant	0.6791***	0.6755***	0.5243***	0.5169***
	[0.115]	[0.113]	[0.090]	[0.089]
Observations	838	838	799	781
instruments	36	37	103	118
Overall	141	141	140	140
Arellano-Bond: AR(1)	0.00	0.00	0.00	0.00
Arellano-Bond: AR(2)	0.1489	0.1506	0.1087	0.0705
Sargan Test (p-Val)	0.0959	0.0901	0.0043	0.0526

The dependent variable is shadow economy (LSE). L.LSE is the lag of shadow economy. All the other variables include (LU) unemployment, (LT) trade, (LGDP) gross domestic product, government expenditure (LGE), (LPS) political stability, (LRQ) regulation quality, (D1) dummy variable, (LDC) domestic credit to private sector, and (LDC_D1) interaction of domestic credit to private sector with dummy variable. For detailed descriptions, refer to section 6.3.1 and the variables summary Table A9 in Appendices. Standard errors are in parentheses and * $p < 0.1$, ** $p < 0.05$, *** $p < 0.01$ denote significance at 10%, 5%, and 1%, respectively.

economy (LSE). All the diagnostic tests are satisfied. In specification model (4), which is the baseline regression, we include interactive terms (LDC*D1). The coefficient of financial development is negatively significant, which suggests that financial development reduces shadow economy. But the coefficient of interactive term (−0.0092) proposes that the impact of financial development in case of OIC countries is small compared to non-OIC countries. We can calculate the coefficient of domestic credit to private sector (LDC) for OIC countries, that is, (−0.0264 + 0.0172 = −0.0092) compared to the coefficient of domestic credit to private sector (LDC) in non-OIC countries (−0.0264). In other words, the effect of domestic credit to private sector (LDC) in the model (4) is negative on shadow economy in both OIC and the non-OIC countries. However, the effect is lower in

86 *Results and Discussion*

OIC countries. These findings provide empirical support that predicts the negative relationship between financial development and shadow economy. These findings are in line with Berdiev and Saunoris (2016) and Bayar and Ozturk (2016), as they reported that increase in financial development reduces shadow economy. However, the lower impact in case of OIC countries may be because of the fact that the majority of OIC member nations are developing countries and the financial outlook of the OIC member countries 2017 mentions that OIC economies performs worse than the world average in terms of financial development. Therefore, it may take time to bring additional people into the formal financial system from shadow economy.

7.6 Financial Inclusion and Shadow Economy

In Tables 7.6 and 7.7, we observe that the selection of dynamic model has justified as the lag coefficients of the dependent variables in all models' specifications are significant at 1%. Similarly, overidentification restrictions are also found to be correct as confirmed by Hansen test. Likewise, the tests of autocorrelation, that is, AR (1) and AR (2), also pass the diagnostic tests.

7.6.1 The Effect of Financial Inclusion on Shadow Economy

In this section, we explore the influence of financial inclusion on shadow economy. Tables 7.6 and 7.7 show the result of GMM regression, which is the baseline regression while the fixed effect and random effect results are provided in appendices. The dependent variable is shadow economy (LSE). All the diagnostic tests of autocorrelation and instruments overidentifications have passed, while the dynamic of our model is passed as lag dependent variable is significant.

In both Tables 7.6 and 7.7, we see that there is negative association between financial inclusion and shadow economy. In Table 7.6 in the first part, model (1) is our baseline model, where we have used interactive term (OIC dummy (D1) with automated teller machines (LATM)). The coefficient of financial inclusion, that is, automated teller machines (LATM) is negatively significant, which shows that the impact of financial inclusion on shadow economy is negative. On the other hand, for OIC countries, the coefficient of automated teller machines (LATM) can be calculated as ($-0.0275 + 0.0217 = -0.0058$), which is smaller than the coefficient of automated teller machines (LATM) per 100,000 adults in non-OIC countries (-0.0275). It means that an increase in automated teller machines (LATM) reduces shadow economy but the effect is less in OIC countries. Similarly, in Table 7.7 in models (4), (5), (6), we have interacted (OIC dummy (D1)) with bank deposits (LBD)). The coefficient of bank deposits (LBD) for OIC countries can be calculated as ($0.0490-0.1007 = -0.0517$) compared to -0.1007 of non-OIC nations. This result also predicts that bank deposits impact shadow economy inversely, but in case of OIC economies, the influence is less.

Next, we move to Table 7.7, where the first three models – model (1), model (2), and model (3) – represent bank branches per 100,000 adults' (LBB) results

Results and Discussion 87

and the second three models – model (4), model (5), and model (6) – are representing results of bank credit to bank deposits (%) (LBCBD) coefficients. Focusing on model (1), we see that bank branches (LBB) are negatively associated with shadow economy while the coefficient of interactive term (D1 dummy with bank branches (LBB)) reveals that the impact of financial inclusion on shadow economy in OIC economies is less, that is, ($-0.0616 + 0.0360 = -0.0256$) compared to -0.0616 of non-OIC countries. Similarly, after interaction of OIC dummy with bank credit to bank deposits (%) (LBCBD) in model (4), we have found negatively ($-0.1243 + 0.1048 = -0.0195$) significant coefficient, which is also consistent with other proxies that the impact of financial inclusion on shadow economy is less in case of OIC countries compared to non-OIC.

These findings predict negative relationship between financial inclusion and the shadow economy. The small coefficients of financial inclusion in the case of OIC countries may be justified that financial system in OIC member countries are not much developed compared to non-OIC countries. which can also be supported by the subsequent figures, that is, Figures 7.1 to 7.14. Similarly, another possible reason for lower effects in case of OIC countries may be that the majority of the population in OIC economies are Muslim, while the available financial system is conventional, which is not in line with their religious beliefs. They might be financially excluded by choice, as Kim et al. (2018) mentioned:

> Muslims, who make up around 1/4 of the world's population, voluntarily allow themselves to be financially excluded. The reason for this is that the current financial system goes against the system of Islamic religious rules called Shari'a. In recent decades, however, thanks to the emergence of Shari'a-complaint financial products and insurances, which allow for financial exceptions in accordance with a flexible interpretation of Shari'a, which play a significant role in improving of the level of financial inclusion of Islamic countries.

Therefore, financial inclusion may not be that effective in reducing shadow economy in OIC countries compared to non-OIC countries.

In Tables 7.6 and 7.7, the coefficient of financial inclusion is small in the case of OIC countries. This small coefficient can be supported by the subsequent Figures from 7.1 to 7.8.

In Figure 7.1 we see that the marginal effect of bank deposit on shadow economy in OIC countries is less compared to non-OIC countries. It means that the impact of bank deposit on shadow economy in OIC counties is less (-0.05) compared to non-OIC countries (-0.10). The coefficient for OIC and non-OIC can be calculated as taking derivative of shadow economy with respect to bank deposit, that is, $\dfrac{\partial se}{\partial bd} = \beta_1 + \beta_2$ where β_1 is the coefficient of bank deposit while β_2 is the coefficient of interaction term (BD*D1). So, to estimate the marginal effect for non-OIC countries where OIC dummy (D1) = 0, we estimate the following equation.

Table 7.6 Financial inclusion and shadow economy using proxies of ATMs per 100,000 adults and bank deposit (% of GDP)

Dependent Var SE	(1)	(2)	(3)	(4)	(5)	(6)
L.LSE	0.8333***	0.8353***	0.8491***	0.7728***	0.7881***	0.7882***
	[0.076]	[0.071]	[0.071]	[0.064]	[0.061]	[0.062]
LMS	−0.1669***	−0.1706***	−0.1684***	−0.1650**	−0.2148**	−0.2151**
	[0.064]	[0.063]	[0.059]	[0.064]	[0.089]	[0.091]
YEAR	0.0002	0.0003	0.0005	−0.0009**	−0.0011**	−0.0010*
	[0.001]	[0.001]	[0.001]	[0.000]	[0.001]	[0.001]
LGDPP	−0.0988*	−0.1027*	−0.1001*	−0.1409**	−0.1287**	−0.1329**
	[0.056]	[0.059]	[0.056]	[0.066]	[0.065]	[0.068]
LTAX				0.0566**	0.0637**	0.0608**
				[0.025]	[0.029]	[0.029]
LMF				−0.023		
				[0.065]		
LU					−0.0347*	−0.0350*
					[0.020]	[0.020]
D1	−0.0218*	−0.0212*	−0.0231*	−0.0592*	−0.0772**	−0.0787**
	[0.012]	[0.012]	[0.014]	[0.033]	[0.032]	[0.034]
LATM	**−0.0275****	**−0.0283****	**−0.0278****			
	[0.013]	**[0.013]**	**[0.014]**			
D1*LATM	**0.0217***	**0.0211***	**0.0212***			
	[0.011]	**[0.011]**	**[0.011]**			
D1*LBD				**0.0490****	**0.0615*****	**0.0635*****
				[0.024]	**[0.022]**	**[0.024]**
LBD				**−0.1007*****	**−0.1048*****	**−0.1106*****
				[0.034]	**[0.031]**	**[0.033]**

Constant	0.7598	0.6357	0.3607	2.7706***	3.3558***	3.1438***
	[0.942]	[0.858]	[0.890]	[0.866]	[1.135]	[1.161]
Observations	1141	1141	1130	1196	1199	1199
instruments	19	19	19	26	23	23
Overall	122	122	121	121	120	120
Arellano-Bond: AR(1)	0.00	0.00	0.00	0.00	0.00	0.00
Arellano-Bond: AR(2)	0.0691	0.0734	0.0629	0.5872	0.6481	0.6231
Hansen (p-Val)	0.5677	0.5508	0.6312	0.9154	0.5348	0.4911

The dependent variable is shadow economy (LSE). L.LSE is the lag of shadow economy. All the other variables include (LMS) money supply, (year) time variable, (LGDPP) GDP per capita, (LTAX) tax, (LMF) monetary freedom, (LU) unemployment, (D1) dummy variable, (LATM) automated teller machines per 100,000 adults, (D1*LATM) interaction of dummy variable with automated teller machines per 100,000 adults, (D1*LBD) interaction of dummy variable with bank deposits, (LBD) bank deposits. For detailed descriptions, refer to section 6.3.1 and the variables summary table A9 in Appendices. Standard errors are in parentheses and * p < 0.1, ** p < 0.05, *** p < 0.01 denote significance at 10%, 5%, and 1%, respectively.

Table 7.7 Financial inclusion and shadow economy using proxies of bank branches per 100,000 adults and bank credit to bank deposits (%)

Dependent Var SE	(1)	(2)	(3)	(4)	(5)	(6)
L.LSE	0.7725***	0.7850***	0.7726***	0.8103***	0.7935***	0.7831***
	[0.073]	[0.070]	[0.097]	[0.084]	[0.090]	[0.052]
LTAX	0.0827**	0.0822**	0.0886**	0.0499**	0.0592**	0.0795***
	[0.041]	[0.040]	[0.043]	[0.024]	[0.030]	[0.028]
LU	0.0003	−0.0004	−0.0021	−0.016		
	[0.012]	[0.012]	[0.013]	[0.013]		
LT	−0.0416			−0.0446	−0.0457	−0.0494*
	[0.028]			[0.029]	[0.030]	[0.026]
YEAR	−0.0015**	−0.0017***	−0.0020***	−0.0015**	−0.0016**	−0.0018***
	[0.001]	[0.001]	[0.001]	[0.001]	[0.001]	[0.001]
LGDPP	−0.1286**	−0.1182***	−0.0990***	−0.1232*	−0.1237*	−0.1418*
	[0.062]	[0.045]	[0.025]	[0.074]	[0.073]	[0.084]
LMS	−0.1624*	−0.1774**	−0.2459***	−0.0888	−0.0894	−0.1198
	[0.093]	[0.075]	[0.092]	[0.081]	[0.078]	[0.087]
LMF		−0.0185				
		[0.023]				
D1	−0.0224*	−0.0206	−0.0115	−0.1909*	−0.2229**	−0.1833**
	[0.013]	[0.014]	[0.014]	[0.098]	[0.102]	[0.071]
LBB	**−0.0616*****	**−0.0651*****	**−0.0555****			
	[0.023]	**[0.023]**	**[0.026]**			
D1*LBB	**0.0360****	**0.0371****	**0.0238**			
	[0.017]	**[0.017]**	**[0.018]**			
LBCBD				**−0.1243***	**−0.1302****	**−0.1069*****
				[0.063]	**[0.063]**	**[0.036]**

D1*LBCBD						
D1*LBCBD				0.1048**	0.1226**	0.1043***
				[0.051]	[0.054]	[0.038]
Constant	4.0315***	4.2882***	5.0809***	3.9748**	4.2213**	4.6473***
	[1.473]	[1.349]	[1.769]	[1.620]	[1.654]	[1.371]
Observations	1162	1156	1162	1193	1203	1195
instruments	24	27	27	24	23	27
Overall	120	120	120	120	121	121
Arellano-Bond: AR(1)	0.00	0.00	0.00	0.00	0.00	0.00
Arellano-Bond: AR(2)	0.5828	0.6617	0.9635	0.306	0.3326	0.5065
Hansen Test (p-Val)	0.1009	0.2768	0.3216	0.3933	0.4079	0.4523

The dependent variable is shadow economy (LSE). L.LSE is the lag of shadow economy. All the other variables include (LTAX) tax, (LU) unemployment, (LT) trade, (year) time variable, (LGDPP) GDP per capita, (LMS) money supply, (LMF) monetary freedom, (D1) dummy variable, (LBB) bank branches per 100,000 adults, (D1*LBB) interaction of dummy variable with bank branches per 100,000 adults, (LBCBD) bank credit to bank deposits, and (D1* LBCBD) interaction of dummy variable with bank credit to bank deposits. For detailed descriptions, refer to section 6.3.1 and the variables summary table A9 in Appendices. Standard errors are in parentheses and * $p < 0.1$, ** $p < 0.05$, *** $p < 0.01$ denote significance at 10%, 5%, and 1%, respectively.

92 Results and Discussion

$$\frac{\partial se}{\partial bd} = \beta_1 + \beta_2 \left(OICdummy \left(D1 \right) = 0 \right)$$

$$\frac{\partial se}{\partial bd} = \beta_1 + \left(\beta_2 * 0 \right)$$

we get

$$\frac{\partial se}{\partial bd} = \beta_1$$

$$\frac{\partial se}{\partial bd} = -0.10$$

So, the coefficient of $\beta_1 = -0.10$, which we got from Figure 7.1 in case of non-OIC countries.

Similarly, we can calculate the coefficient for OIC countries

$$\frac{\partial se}{\partial bd} = \beta_1 + \beta_2 \text{ when OIC dummy (D1)} = 1$$

$$\frac{\partial se}{\partial bd} = \beta_1 + \beta_2 \left(OICdummy \left(D1 \right) = 1 \right)$$

$$\frac{\partial se}{\partial bd} = \beta_1 + \left(\beta_2 * 1 \right)$$

So, we get

$$\frac{\partial se}{\partial bd} = \beta_1 + \beta_2$$

$$\frac{\partial se}{\partial bd} = -0.10 + 0.05 \left(1 \right)$$

$$\frac{\partial se}{\partial bd} = -0.05$$

So, the coefficient for OIC countries is -0.05 compared to non-OIC countries, which is -0.10. Therefore, the impact of bank deposit is less and smaller on shadow economy in the case of OIC countries compared to non-OIC countries.

In Figure 7.2 we see that the marginal effect of number of ATMs on shadow economy in OIC countries is less (-0.01) compared to non-OIC countries (-0.03),

Results and Discussion 93

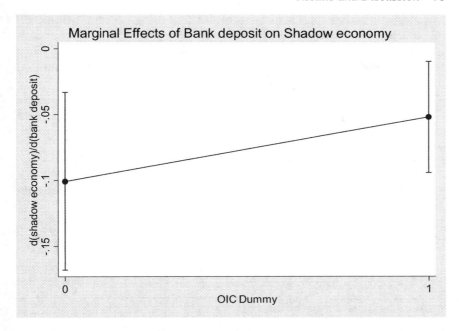

Figure 7.1 Marginal effect of bank deposit on shadow economy
Source: author's own derivation

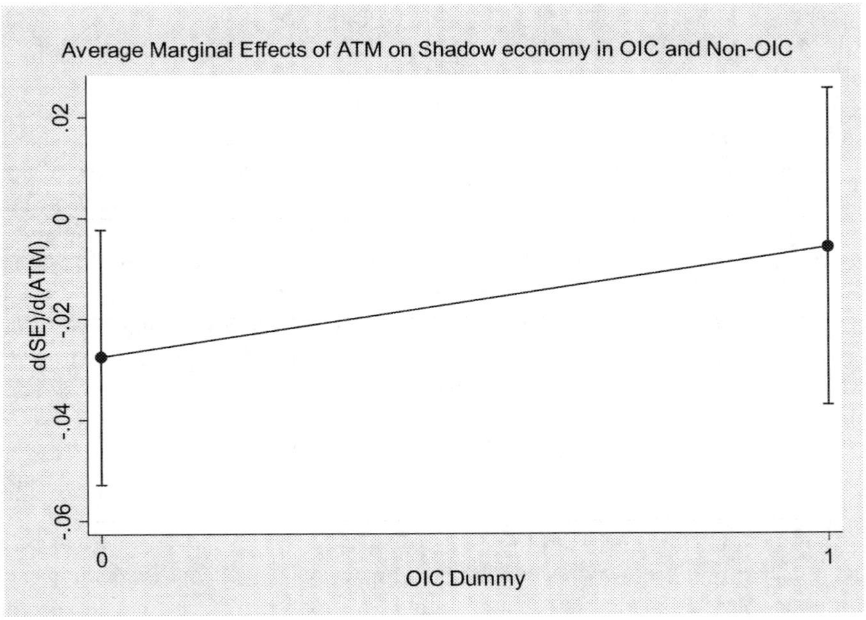

Figure 7.2 Marginal effect of number of ATMs on shadow economy
Source: author's own derivation

94 *Results and Discussion*

which shows that the impact of numbers of ATMs on shadow economy is small in OIC countries compared to non-OIC countries.

As we observe in Figure 7.3, the marginal effect of bank branch on shadow economy in OIC countries is less (-0.03) compared to non-OIC (-0.07) predicting small impact of bank branch on shadow economy in OIC economies compared to non-OIC nations.

As we observe in Figure 7.4, the marginal effect of bank credit to bank deposit on shadow economy in OIC countries is less (-0.05) compared to non-OIC countries (-0.15), indicating bank credit to bank deposit impact is small on shadow economy in OIC economies compared to non-OIC.

Figure 7.5 shows that the marginal effect of bank deposit on shadow economy is decreasing from ($-.05$) to (0.05) in the case of OIC countries compared to non-OIC countries.

In Figure 7.6, at the point -0.10 is the marginal effect of bank deposit on shadow economy in case of non-OIC countries while at the point -0.05 is the marginal effect of bank deposit on shadow economy in case of OIC countries.

Figure 7.7 shows the movement of the predictive values of bank deposit with respect to shadow economy. We see that all the values are significant at 95% level of alpha because none of them crosses zero. Similarly, we also see that the negative impact of bank deposit on shadow economy in case of non-OIC countries is higher (left upper line is falling sharply) compared to OIC countries (left down line falling slowly).

In Figure 7.8, we see that the impact of bank deposit on shadow economy is deeper in the case of non-OIC countries as compared to OIC countries.

Figure 7.9 represents the association between shadow economy and number of ATMs for full sample, where the slope of the line is downward, indicating negative relationship between the number of ATMs and shadow economy.

In the case of non-OIC countries, Figure 7.10, the slope of the line is negative, too, and sharply fallen, which shows a strong negative correlation between both variables.

On the other hand, in the case of OIC countries in Figure 7.11, the slope of the line is negative, too, but not sharply fallen, which shows relatively weak negative correlation between shadow economy and number of ATMs. This association provides support to the estimated coefficient that the impact of number of ATMs in the case of OIC countries is small compared to non-OIC countries.

In Figure 7.12, we see the association between shadow economy and bank credit to bank deposit for full sample where the slope of the line is downward, which indicates a negative relationship between bank credit to bank deposit and shadow economy.

In Figure 7.13 we see that the slope of the line is negative, too, and sharply fallen, which shows a strong inverse correlation between both variables in the case of non-OIC countries.

In case of OIC countries, in Figure 7.14, the slope of the line is negative, too, but not sharply fallen, which shows a relatively weak inverse correlation between both variables. This weak association provides support to the estimated coefficient for OIC countries where the coefficient is small in case of OIC countries compared to non-OIC countries.

Results and Discussion 95

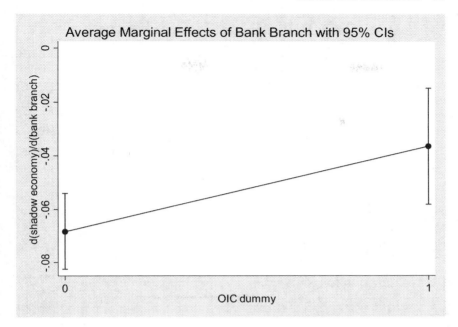

Figure 7.3 Marginal effect of bank branch on shadow economy
Source: author's own derivation

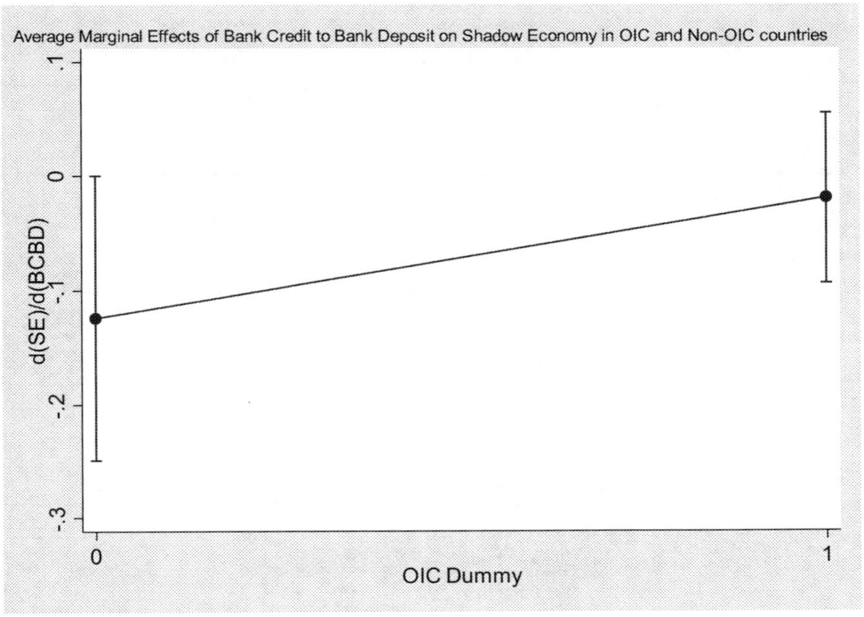

Figure 7.4 Marginal effect of bank credit to bank deposit on shadow economy
Source: author's own derivation

96 *Results and Discussion*

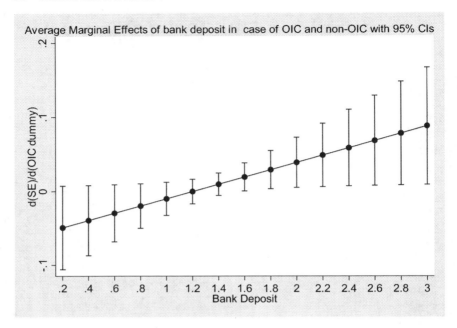

Figure 7.5 Marginal effect of bank deposit on shadow economy in case of full sample
Source: author's own derivation

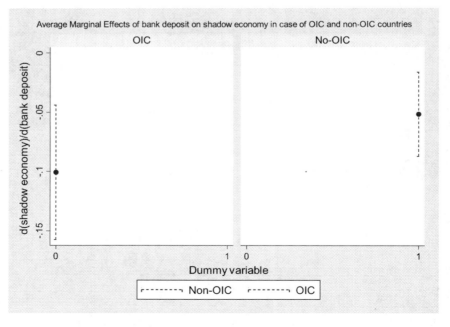

Figure 7.6 Marginal effect of bank deposit on shadow economy in case of OIC and non-OIC countries
Source: author's own derivation

Results and Discussion 97

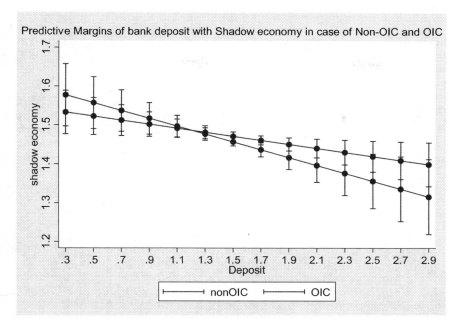

Figure 7.7 Margin predictive values of bank deposit with respect to shadow economy for OIC and non-OIC countries

Source: author's own derivation

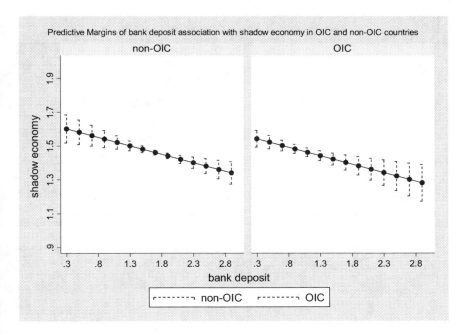

Figure 7.8 Margin predictive values of bank deposit on shadow economy for OIC and non-OIC countries

Source: author's own derivation

98 *Results and Discussion*

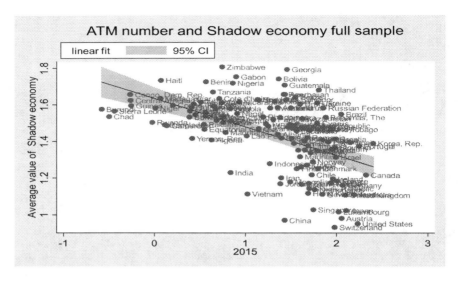

Figure 7.9 Association between ATM number and shadow economy in full sample
Source: author's own derivation

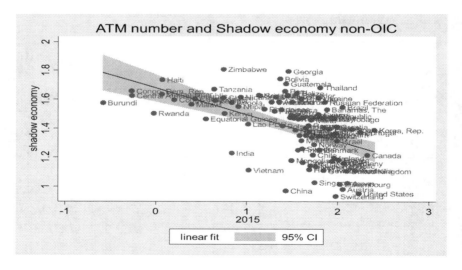

Figure 7.10 Association between ATM number and shadow economy in non-OIC countries
Source: author's own derivation

Results and Discussion 99

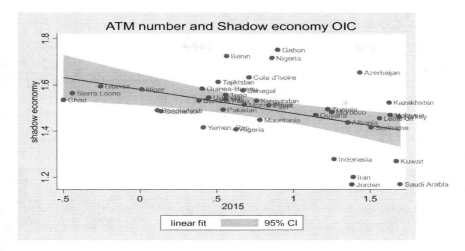

Figure 7.11 Association between ATM number and shadow economy in OIC countries
Source: author's own derivation

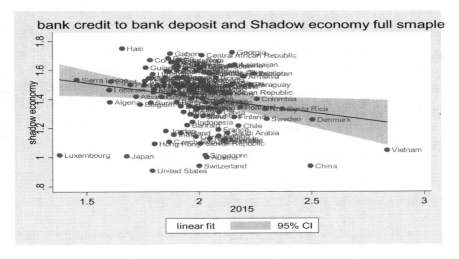

Figure 7.12 Association between bank credit to bank deposit and shadow economy in full sample
Source: author's own derivation

100 Results and Discussion

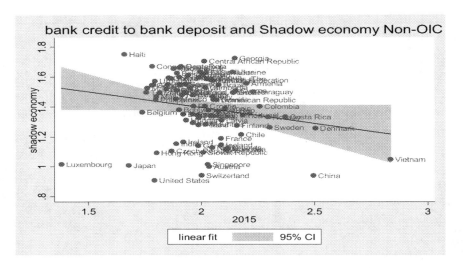

Figure 7.13 Association between bank credit to bank deposit and shadow economy in non-OIC countries

Source: author's own derivation

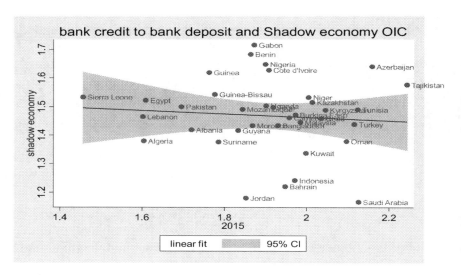

Figure 7.14 Association between bank credit to bank deposit and shadow economy in OIC countries

Source: author's own derivation

Results and Discussion 101

7.7 Robustness Checks

7.7.1 Full Sample and Subsamples

For robustness purposes, we employ GMM and fixed effect and random effect in the case of a full sample as well as for the subsamples. The results, reported in the Appendices (A1 to A5), reveal consistent coefficients across different models.

7.7.2 An Alternative Measure of Institution Variables

As an additional robustness, alternative proxies of the institution variables are used. The results, reported in Tables A1 to A3a (Appendices), provide evidence of consistent results across different models.

The coefficients of interactive terms are provided in Table 7.8. To check the significance of the coefficients, we reject H_0 and conclude that all the interactive terms are statistically significant. For more details, see Appendices (Tables A6 to A8). Furthermore, Table 7.9 shows the difference between OIC and non-OIC countries with respect to shadow economy. A majority of variables show that there is no significant difference between OIC and non-OIC countries. Similarly, comparing mean in Table 7.10, it can be inferred that a majority of the variables are close to each other, indicating similarity between both groups of nations.

7.8 Conclusion

The key findings can be summarized as follows. First, GDP is weakly and negatively associated with shadow economy. This finding is consistent with prior studies (Schneider and Enste, 2000 and Dell'Anno and Schneider, 2003), providing evidence that an increase in gross domestic product reduces shadow

Table 7.8 Interactive terms

Var	Coefficients name	Interactive term	p-value
1	Bank deposits to GDP (%)	D1*LBD + LBD = 0	0.0095
2	Automated teller machines (ATMs)	D1*LATM + LATM = 0	0.0416
3	Domestic credit to private sector (% of GDP)	D1*LDC+ LDC = 0	0.0425

In Table 7.8, D1 is dummy variable, LBD is the log of bank deposit, LATM is the log of automated teller machines (LATM) per 100,000 adults, LDC is the domestic credit to private sector (%). For detailed descriptions, refer to section 6.3.1 and the variables summary Table A9 in Appendices.

Table 7.9 Testing level of significance between OIC and non-OIC countries

LGDP	−0.565
LGE	1.127
LROL	1.169
LRQ	2.71**

102　*Results and Discussion*

Table 7.10 Comparative mean of variables

Variable	Non-OIC	OIC
LSE	1.413303	1.487896
LGDP	1.605262	1.618079
LMS	1.837652	1.846334
LGE	1.180590	1.117413
LGDPP	1.593308	1.590572
LT	1.921869	1.865407
LTAX	−0.789833	−0.993674
LU	0.800957	0.854386
LPS	1.626033	1.326984
LRQ	1.687993	1.501308
LROL	1.631201	1.429672
LECOF	1.794591	1.749997
LBF	1.824609	1.747523
LATM	1.485362	0.887854
LBD	1.619941	1.447176
LBB	1.132031	0.722500
LBCBD	1.988422	1.872867
LDCPS	1.652168	1.349298
LMF	1.864104	1.871705
LTF	1.875272	1.818767
LINF	1.618342	1.614213
LVA	1.675328	1.385239

The variables include (LSE) shadow economy, (LGDP) gross domestic product, money supply (LMS), government expenditure (LGE), GDP per capita (LGDPP), trade (LT), tax (LTAX), unemployment (LU), (LPS) political stability, (LRQ) regulation quality, (LROL) rule of law, (LECOF) economic freedom, (LBF) business freedom, (LATM) automated teller machines per 100,000 adults, (LBD) bank deposits to GDP, (LBB) bank branches per 100,000 adults, (LBCBD) bank credit to bank deposits, (LDCPS) domestic credit to private sector, monetary freedom (LMF), (LTF) trade freedom, inflation (LINF), and voice and accountability (LVA). For detailed descriptions, see section 6.3.1 and the variables summary Table A9 in Appendices.

economy, but this negative impact, even though it is statistically significant, is economically insignificant because the coefficient is very small. Hence, such insignificant association of GDP with shadow economy is in line with the Dualist school, which believes that both official economy and shadow economy are totally isolated from each other (Hart, 1973; ILO, 1972 and Rothenberg et al., 2016). Second, government expenditure increases the size of shadow economy. This result is in line with Dell'Anno et al. (2018) and Schneider et al. (2010). They reported that government spending increases shadow economy as it distorts resources allocation. Similarly, according to Nikopour and Habibullah (2010), increased government size may distort the economic and political environment and crowd out private investments. In a recent study, Fedotenkov and Schneider (2017) found that military expenditure increases shadow economy because of improper use of budget resources. Furthermore, this result is also supported by the neoclassical school of thought, which believes that an increased government involvement in the economy might distort the economic environment of business and discourage and crowd out private sector investments.

Third, institutional quality is negatively related to shadow economy. This finding is like prior studies (Elbahnasawy et al., 2016; Torgler and Schneider, 2007 and Dreher et al., 2009). This negative effect appears to suggest that countries having good institutional quality are more likely to have a small size of shadow economy. Fourth, the relationship between financial development and shadow economy is negative even though the impact is small in the case of OIC countries. This result is supported by the previous studies (Berdiev and Saunoris, 2016, and Bayar and Ozturk, 2016). Precisely, the earlier literature reveals that an increase in financial development decreases shadow economy. The small effect of financial development on shadow economy in the case of OIC economies may be due to the underdeveloped financial market of these countries, as a majority of OIC member nations are developing countries. Finally, financial inclusion is negatively associated with shadow economy, but the effect is less in OIC countries. One plausible explanation is that in OIC countries, a majority of the population is Muslim, but the financial system of these countries is not Islamic, and therefore not in line with their religious beliefs. Therefore, they might be voluntarily allowing themselves to be financially excluded. This argument is consistent with Kim et al. (2018).

Notes

1 Part of the content is published as an article (Determinants of Shadow Economy in OIC and Non-OIC Countries: The Role of Financial Development, *International Journal of Emerging Markets* (2021)).
2 Part of the content is published as an article (Macroeconomic Fundamentals, Institutional Quality and Shadow Economy in OIC and Non-OIC Countries, *Journal of Economic Studies* (2022)).

8 Inferences and Policy Implications

This study aimed to investigate shadow economy in detail, that is, the determinants of the shadow economy, the impact of financial development on shadow economy, and the role of financial inclusion in shadow economy. In reviewing the literature, we have discussed in detail the controversies regarding shadow economy. It is realized that shadow economy has a sophisticated and latent nature. Historically speaking, this phenomenon has been observed since the middle of the twentieth century but was discovered and properly recognized in academic circles by Keith Hart (1971) and ILO (1972).

We also explored types, characteristics, historical development, Islamic view, and the size of shadow economy around the world. It is well-known that most of the OIC economies are developing, and one of the important issues in developing economies regarding formulating economic policies is the nonexistence of efficient, timely, accurate, reliable, and consistent data on one hand, while, on the other hand, there is a huge portion of shadow economy, that is, 34.36% in OIC states, that is not recognized in national statistics. Even though national statistics are available and in line with the national account system, still it deteriorates in terms of inaccuracy and deficiency of valuation of economic variables and economic activities. Similarly, in these countries, data collection is problematic and estimation methods suffer from deficiency. In these countries, firms and businesses keep information secret from government authorities because of involvement in illicit and shadow activities. Authenticity and accuracy of economic statistics and data are important to implement and formulate efficient and effective economic policies and allocate resources in a proper way. So, if the size of shadow economy is large, it creates governance problems, signaling the presence of excessive regulations, understates national income and other macroeconomic variables. If macroeconomic variables present wrong information, then the policies based on such variables will also be incorrect and inefficient.

It can also be concluded that shadow economy exists in all types of economies in different shapes and in unlikely places. Many researchers and economists have studied shadow economy from different perspectives by using different methodologies and achieving distinct objectives because of the complex, dynamic, and heterogenous nature of present-day economies (Becker, 2004 and Schneider, 2005). However, characteristics, nature, determinants, and size of shadow

DOI: 10.4324/9781003329954-8

Inferences and Policy Implications   105

economy differ from country to country. Researchers have studied shadow economy in advanced and transaction countries, while less concentration has been given to developing countries. It is also realized that there is a knowledge gap regarding shadow economy in the context of OIC countries.

Based on the literature, it can be concluded that shadow economy exists in all types of economies in different shapes. However, characteristics, nature, determinants, and size of shadow economies differ from country to country.

While exploring the determinants of shadow economy, GDP is found to be a weak determining factor, which suggests that both sectors, that is, official economy and shadow economy are isolated from each other. Therefore, economic growth does not necessarily decrease the size of shadow economy. Government should be rational while allocating economic resources, because misallocation of economic resources may push more people toward shadow economy. Shadow economy is found to have a negative correlation with institutional quality, which suggests that good institutional setup can attract firms and businesses from informal sector to the official economy.

We also investigated the impact of financial development on shadow economy. The coefficient of financial development is found to be negatively significant, which suggests that as financial development increases, the size of shadow economy decreases, even though the effect is small in the case of OIC countries. Therefore, it is suggested that the financial system should be improved. The governments of OIC countries may consider financial development while making plans about shadow economy, even though this a not a strong tool because the coefficient of financial development in the case of OIC countries is small.

Similarly, we found that financial inclusion reduced shadow economy, although the impact is small in OIC economies. So, the governments need to put forward policies that bring in those who are excluded by choice.

8.1 Policy Implications

From a fiscal policy perspective, shadow economy reduces government revenue and results in higher and more costly public expenditure. In order to manage expenditure, it is important for the government to know the size of shadow economy to overcome such problems. Keeping in view all these issues, it is discovered that shadow economy is one of the main challenges and an important concern for policy makers. If the size of shadow economy is large, it creates governance problems, signals the presence of excessive regulations, and understates national income and other macroeconomic variables. If macroeconomic variables deliver the wrong information, the policies based on such variables will also be incorrect and inefficient. Therefore, consideration of shadow economy while making economic policies is essential.

There is a need for special consideration of shadow economy in socioeconomic policies. In the same way, formalization in the labor and goods market through establishing good institutions is very important. Rationalization of resources should be one of the main concerns while formulating policies, especially

106 *Inferences and Policy Implications*

considering shadow economy. Likewise, based on the results of the impact of financial development and financial inclusion on the shadow economy, OIC member countries should consider financial progress one of the main agendas.

So, the key implication of this study is to improve the quality of institutions, because economic growth, financial development, and financial inclusion coefficients are not strong enough in the case of OIC countries to reduce the size of shadow economy despite negative association.

The significant size of shadow economy can lead to macroeconomic, microeconomic, and social problems. Macroeconomic policy can be less effective and thus, in turn, can make it harder for the policy makers to get macroeconomic stability. Furthermore, in the presence of a large shadow economy, official statistics will present the wrong picture of the economy. As far as the microeconomic aspects are concerned, shadow economy creates distortions in resource allocation. It can be concluded that to reduce unfair competition among the official economy players and to increase government revenue, transformation of business enterprises and attracting entrepreneurs from shadow economy to official economy are crucial. Similarly, based on the findings of the study, the only way to have a small shadow economy is to have good institutional setup.

In order to set up comprehensive economic policies framework, this study can be used as a guideline to consider shadow economy along with official economy. Similarly, the identification of the determinants of shadow economy also help governments to understand the reasons for the existence of shadow economy and how to use each indicator. Empirical findings of financial development can be used to reduce shadow economy through financial market development. Likewise, financial inclusion results can help to make appropriate policies for reducing financial exclusion by reducing shadow economy. More importantly, good institutions setup is the key to address the issue of shadow economy. Finally, the findings of this study can be used as the basis for future studies.

Appendices

Table A1 Determinants of shadow economy using rule of law

Dependent variable SE	Full sample			Subsample OIC			Subsample non-OIC		
	(1) FE	*(2)* RE	*(3)* GMM	*(1)* FE	*(2)* RE	*(3)* GMM	*(1)* FE	*(2)* RE	*(3)* GMM
LECOF	0.0911** [0.036]	0.0878** [0.035]	-0.0849** [0.037]	0.0534 [0.048]	0.0552 [0.046]	-0.0980 [0.073]	0.1209** [0.050]	0.1158** [0.049]	0.0985*** [0.024]
LTF	-0.0889*** [0.034]	-0.0856*** [0.033]	0.0602** [0.027]	-0.0446 [0.041]	-0.0457 [0.039]	-0.0275 [0.026]	-0.1255** [0.048]	-0.1211*** [0.046]	-0.0919*** [0.022]
LT	-0.1566*** [0.028]	-0.1490*** [0.027]	-0.1370*** [0.048]	-0.2240*** [0.046]	-0.2203*** [0.043]	-0.1021*** [0.030]	-0.1051*** [0.033]	-0.0970*** [0.032]	-0.0912*** [0.022]
LGDP	-0.0002** [0.000]	-0.0002** [0.000]	-0.0016*** [0.001]	-0.0001** [0.001]	0.0000** [0.001]	-0.0018** [0.002]	-0.0000 [0.000]	-0.0001** [0.000]	-0.0026*** [0.001]
LGE	0.1631*** [0.036]	0.1506*** [0.034]	0.0967*** [0.023]	0.1813*** [0.058]	0.1616*** [0.055]	0.0596* [0.032]	0.1491*** [0.044]	0.1402*** [0.041]	0.0214 [0.027]
LMS	0.0291** [0.014]	0.0303** [0.015]	-0.0389** [0.018]	0.0201 [0.028]	0.0189 [0.028]	-0.0176 [0.021]	0.0324** [0.013]	0.0340** [0.013]	0.0406*** [0.015]
LROL	-0.0974*** [0.011]	-0.1032*** [0.011]	-0.1294*** [0.037]	-0.0906*** [0.017]	-0.0943*** [0.017]	-0.0877*** [0.020]	-0.1047*** [0.013]	-0.1103*** [0.013]	-0.1021*** [0.015]
L.LSE			0.8099*** [0.093]			0.7195*** [0.104]			0.6036*** [0.048]
Constant	1.6615*** [0.063]	1.6688*** [0.064]	0.7271*** [0.246]	1.7999*** [0.107]	1.8199*** [0.097]	0.9294*** [0.258]	1.5880*** [0.073]	1.5920*** [0.076]	0.8370*** [0.089]
Observations	975	975	838	294	294	252	681	681	586
Adjusted R^2	0.457			0.449			0.477		
instruments			14			43			24

(Continued)

Table A1 (Continued)

Dependent variable SE	Full sample			Subsample OIC			Subsample non-OIC		
	(1)	(2)	(3)	(1)	(2)	(3)	(1)	(2)	(3)
	FE	RE	GMM	FE	RE	GMM	FE	RE	GMM
overall	141	141	141	42	42	42	99	99	99
Arellano-Bond: AR(1)			0.00			0.00			0.00
Arellano-Bond: AR(2)			0.8203			0.0716			0.9754
Hansen Test (p-Val)			0.5830			0.3305			0.0000
F-Stats (p-Val)			0.0000			0.0000			0.0000

The dependent variable is shadow economy (LSE). (L.LSE) is the lag of shadow economy. All the other variables include (LECOF) economic freedom, (LTF) trade freedom, trade (T), (LGDP) gross domestic product, government expenditure (LGE), money supply (LMS), (LROL) rule of law. For detailed descriptions, see section 6.3.1 and the variables summary Table A9. Standard errors are in parentheses and * $p < 0.1$, ** $p < 0.05$, *** $p < 0.01$ denote significance at 10%, 5%, and 1%, respectively.

Table A2 Determinants of shadow economy using political stability

Dependent variable SE	Full sample			Subsample OIC			Subsample non-OIC		
	(1)	(2)	(3)	(1)	(2)	(3)	(1)	(2)	(3)
	FE	RE	GMM	FE	RE	GMM	FE	RE	GMM
LECOF	0.0963**	0.0931**	−0.0647	0.0938*	0.0957*	−0.1763**	0.0819	0.0756	0.0972***
	[0.039]	[0.039]	[0.045]	[0.054]	[0.052]	[0.073]	[0.055]	[0.054]	[0.027]
LTF	−0.0983***	−0.0960***	0.0551	−0.1004**	−0.1035**	−0.0238	−0.0826	−0.0773	−0.0758***
	[0.036]	[0.035]	[0.035]	[0.047]	[0.046]	[0.027]	[0.051]	[0.050]	[0.021]
LT	−0.1794***	−0.1709***	−0.1191***	−0.2334***	−0.2300***	−0.0480	−0.1253***	−0.1154***	−0.1176***
	[0.030]	[0.029]	[0.041]	[0.053]	[0.051]	[0.031]	[0.034]	[0.033]	[0.020]
LGDP	−0.0003**	−0.0003**	−0.0032**	−0.0002	−0.0002	−0.0035**	0.0001	0.0001	−0.0034***

	[0.000]	[0.000]	[0.001]	[0.001]	[0.001]	[0.001]	[0.000]	[0.000]	[0.001]
LGE	0.1495*** [0.036]	0.1347*** [0.034]	0.0568** [0.022]	0.1885*** [0.058]	0.1633*** [0.054]	0.0355 [0.024]	0.1338*** [0.042]	0.1224*** [0.039]	-0.0411* [0.022]
LMS	0.0355** [0.014]	0.0375*** [0.014]	-0.0346* [0.021]	0.0288 [0.028]	0.0284 [0.029]	-0.0115 [0.018]	0.0347*** [0.013]	0.0369*** [0.013]	0.0609*** [0.016]
LPS	-0.0763*** [0.009]	-0.0795*** [0.009]	-0.0536*** [0.020]	-0.0403** [0.016]	-0.0395** [0.016]	-0.0286** [0.011]	-0.1040*** [0.010]	-0.1084*** [0.010]	-0.0539*** [0.009]
L.LSE			0.9903*** [0.053]			0.8930*** [0.064]			0.6507*** [0.051]
Constant	1.6852*** [0.068]	1.6908*** [0.068]	0.3486** [0.141]	1.7582*** [0.118]	1.7819*** [0.105]	0.6571*** [0.216]	1.6274*** [0.082]	1.6293*** [0.084]	0.7666*** [0.094]
Observations	975	975	838	294	294	252	681	681	586
Adjusted R^2	0.412			0.369			0.467		
instruments			14			43			24
overall	141	141	141	42	42	42	99	99	99
Arellano-Bond: AR(1)			0.00			0.00			0.00
Arellano-Bond: AR(2)			0.0542			0.0158			0.2380
Hansen Test (p-Val)			0.1884			0.3242			0.0000
F-Stats (p-Val)			0.0000			0.0000			0.0000

The dependent variable is shadow economy (LSE). (L.LSE) is the lag of shadow economy. All the other variables include (LECOF) economic freedom, (LTF) trade freedom, trade (T), (LGDP) gross domestic product, government expenditure (LGE), money supply (LMS), (LPS) political stability. For detailed descriptions, refer to section 6.3.1 and the variables summary Table A9. Standard errors are in parentheses and * $p < 0.1$, ** $p < 0.05$, *** $p < 0.01$ denote significance at 10%, 5%, and 1%, respectively.

Table A3a Determinants of shadow economy with tax

Dependent variable SE	Full sample			Subsample OIC			Subsample non-OIC		
	(1) FE	(2) RE	(3) GMM	(1) FE	(2) RF	(3) GMM	(1) FE	(2) RE	(3) GMM
L.LSE			0.8238***			0.9881***			0.9036***
			[0.034]			[0.019]			[0.037]
LTAXB	0.0533***	0.0662***	0.0606***	0.0846***	0.0837***	0.0549**	0.0406*	0.0544**	0.0851***
	[0.017]	[0.017]	[0.020]	[0.025]	[0.025]	[0.023]	[0.023]	[0.023]	[0.025]
LMF	0.0017	0.0013	−0.0057	0.0114	0.01	0.0005	−0.004	−0.0052	−0.0459**
	[0.007]	[0.007]	[0.009]	[0.010]	[0.010]	[0.008]	[0.009]	[0.009]	[0.018]
LGDP	−0.0005**	−0.0005**	−0.0031***	−0.0015**	−0.0015**	−0.0044***	−0.0003*	−0.0003**	−0.0036***
	[0.000]	[0.000]	[0.000]	[0.001]	[0.001]	[0.001]	[0.000]	[0.000]	[0.001]
LGE	0.1487***	0.1342***	0.0418***	0.0532***	0.0602**	0.0209**	0.2547***	0.2418***	0.0431**
	[0.019]	[0.019]	[0.011]	[0.025]	[0.024]	[0.008]	[0.029]	[0.029]	[0.018]
LMS	0.0278***	0.0293***	−0.0069	0.0021	0.0025	−0.0043	0.0398***	0.0417***	−0.0287**
	[0.009]	[0.009]	[0.008]	[0.014]	[0.014]	[0.007]	[0.012]	[0.012]	[0.012]
LTF	−0.0661***	−0.0769***	−0.0592***	−0.1005***	−0.0976***	−0.0636***	−0.0471**	−0.0592**	−0.0391
	[0.016]	[0.016]	[0.022]	[0.022]	[0.022]	[0.021]	[0.023]	[0.023]	[0.031]
LROL	−0.1150***	−0.1199***	−0.0679***	−0.0882***	−0.0897***	−0.0208***	−0.1337***	−0.1362***	−0.0449**
	[0.007]	[0.007]	[0.014]	[0.010]	[0.010]	[0.008]	[0.009]	[0.009]	[0.019]
Constant	1.4409***	1.4594***	0.3619***	1.6504***	1.6429***	0.0932***	1.2426***	1.2592***	0.2354***
	[0.029]	[0.032]	[0.059]	[0.038]	[0.040]	[0.036]	[0.050]	[0.053]	[0.067]
Observations	976	976	839	424	424	365	552	552	474
Adjusted R-squared	0.266			0.163			0.399		
Instruments			151			151			99
Overall	141	141	141	62	62	62	79	79	79
Arellano-Bond: AR(1)			0.00			0.00			0.00
Arellano-Bond: AR(2)			0.0171			0.1029			0.0379
Hansen Test (p-Val)			0.5713			.90			0.8669
F-Stats (p-Val)			0.00			0.00			0.00

The dependent variable is shadow economy (LSE). (L.LSE) is the lag of shadow economy. All the other variables include (LTAXB) tax burden, (LMF) monetary freedom, (LGDP) gross domestic product, government expenditure (LGE), money supply (LMS), (LTF) trade freedom, and (LROL) rule of law. For detailed descriptions, refer to section 6.3.1 and the variables summary Table A9. Standard errors are in parentheses and * $p < 0.1$, ** $p < 0.05$, *** $p < 0.01$ denote significance at 10%, 5%, and 1%, respectively.

Table A3b Interaction of OIC dummy (D1 = 1) with bank deposits to GDP (D1*LBD) and automated teller machines (ATMs) per 100,000 adults (D1*LATM)

Dependent variable SE	Bank deposits			Automated teller machines (ATMs)		
	(1)	*(2)*	*(3)*	*(1)*	*(2)*	*(3)*
	FE	*RE*	*GMM*	*FE*	*RE*	*GMM*
LTAX	−0.0637***	−0.0539***	0.0566**			
	[0.013]	[0.013]	[0.025]			
LMF	−0.1050***	−0.1165***	−0.0230			
	[0.029]	[0.028]	[0.065]			
YEAR	−0.0049***	−0.0046***	−0.0009**	−0.0033***	−0.0031***	0.0002
	[0.000]	[0.000]	[0.000]	[0.000]	[0.000]	[0.001]
LGDPP	−0.0699***	−0.0742***	−0.1409**	−0.0833***	−0.0848***	−0.0988*
	[0.010]	[0.010]	[0.066]	[0.010]	[0.010]	[0.056]
LMS	−0.0303**	−0.0297**	−0.1650**	−0.0102	−0.0087	−0.1669***
	[0.013]	[0.013]	[0.064]	[0.012]	[0.012]	[0.064]
L.LSE			0.7728***			0.8333***
			[0.064]			[0.076]
D1	0.0000	−0.0358	−0.0592*	0.0000	0.0181	−0.0218*
	[.]	[0.042]	[0.033]	[.]	[0.033]	[0.012]
LATM				−0.0486***	−0.0527***	−0.0275**
				[0.005]	[0.005]	[0.013]
D1*LATM				0.0173**	0.0181***	0.0217*
				[0.007]	[0.007]	[0.011]
LBD	−0.0731***	−0.0953***	−0.1007***			
	[0.015]	[0.015]	[0.034]			
D1*LBD	0.0443**	0.0489**	0.0490**			
	[0.019]	[0.019]	[0.024]			
LTAXB				−0.0101	0.0067	−0.1994
				[0.041]	[0.040]	[0.307]

(*Continued*)

Table A3b (Continued)

Dependent variable SE	Bank deposits			Automated teller machines (ATMs)		
	(1)	*(2)*	*(3)*	*(1)*	*(2)*	*(3)*
	FE	*RE*	*GMM*	*FE*	*RE*	*GMM*
LEXP				−0.0847***	−0.0876***	−0.0154
				[0.012]	[0.012]	[0.021]
Constant	11.5187***	10.9702***	2.7704***	8.1513***	7.7195***	0.7598
	[0.669]	[0.672]	[0.866]	[0.721]	[0.722]	[0.942]
Observations	1196	1196	1196	1141	1141	1141
Adjusted R^2	0.326			0.350		
instruments			26			19
overall	121	121	121	122	122	122
Arellano-Bond: AR(1)			0.00			0.00
Arellano-Bond: AR(2)			0.5872			0.0691
Hansen (p-Val)			0.9154			0.5677
F-Stats (p-Val)			0.0000			0.0000

The dependent variable is shadow economy (LSE). (L.LSE) is the lag of shadow economy. All the other variables include (LTAX) tax, (LMS) money supply, (year) time variable, (LGDPP) GDP per capita, (LMS) money supply, (D1) dummy variable, (LATM) automated teller machines per 100,000 adults, (D1*LATM) interaction of dummy variable with automated teller machines per 100,000 adults, (LBD) bank deposits, (D1*LBD) interaction of dummy variable with bank deposits (LTAX), tax and export (LEXP). For detailed descriptionsn refer to section 6.3.1 and the variables summary Table A9. Standard errors are in parentheses and * $p < 0.1$, ** $p < 0.05$, *** $p < 0.01$ denote significance at 10%, 5%, and 1%, respectively.

Table A4 Interaction of OIC dummy and bank branches per 100,000 adults' interaction (D1*LBB) and bank credit to bank deposits (%) (D1*LBCBD)

Dependent variable SE	Bank branches			Bank credit to bank deposit		
	(1)	*(2)*	*(3)*	*(1)*	*(2)*	*(3)*
	FE	*RE*	*GMM*	*FE*	*RE*	*GMM*
L.LSE			0.7725***			0.8103***
			[0.073]			[0.084]
LTAX	−0.0379***	−0.0322***	0.0827**	−0.0353***	−0.0327***	0.0499**
	[0.012]	[0.012]	[0.041]	[0.011]	[0.012]	[0.024]

	(1)	(2)	(3)	(4)	(5)	(6)
LU	0.100***	0.0969***	0.0003	0.1043***	0.1009***	-0.016
	(13.71)	(13.22)	[0.012]	[0.008]	[0.008]	[0.013]
LT	-0.147***	-0.145***	-0.0416	-0.1341***	-0.1342***	-0.0446
	(-11.23)	(-11.09)	[0.028]	[0.014]	[0.014]	[0.029]
YEAR	-0.0051***	-0.0050***	-0.0015**	-0.0050***	-0.0049***	-0.0015**
	[0.000]	[0.000]	[0.001]	[0.000]	[0.000]	[0.001]
LGDPP	-0.0758***	-0.0771***	-0.1286**	-0.0627***	-0.0642***	-0.1232*
	[0.009]	[0.010]	[0.062]	[0.009]	[0.009]	[0.074]
LMS	-0.0329***	-0.0311***	-0.1624*	-0.0081	-0.0075	-0.0888
	[0.012]	[0.012]	[0.093]	[0.011]	[0.012]	[0.081]
LMF	-0.1380***	-0.1478***				
	[0.028]	[0.027]				
D1	0.0000	0.0145	-0.0224*	0.0000	-0.0958*	-0.1909*
	[.]	[0.034]	[0.013]	[.]	[0.058]	[0.098]
LBB	-0.0624***	-0.0682***	-0.0616***			
	[0.007]	[0.007]	[0.023]			
D1*LBB	0.0332***	0.0318***	0.0360**			
	[0.012]	[0.012]	[0.017]			
LBCBD				-0.0699***	-0.0781***	-0.1243*
				[0.015]	[0.015]	[0.063]
D1*LBCBD				0.0599**	0.0644**	0.1048**
				[0.025]	[0.025]	[0.051]
Constant	11.9293***	11.7189***	4.0315***	11.5910***	11.5800***	3.9748***
	[0.574]	[0.577]	[1.473]	[0.493]	[0.503]	[1.620]
Observations	1166	1166	1162	1193	1193	1193
Adjusted R^2				0.453		
instruments	121	121	24	120	120	24
overall			120	120	120	120
Arellano-Bond: AR(1)			0.00			0.00
Arellano-Bond: AR(2)			0.5828			0.306
Hansen Test (p-Val)			0.1009			0.3933
F-Stats (p-Val)			0.00			0.00

The dependent variable is shadow economy (LSE). (L.LSE) is the lag of shadow economy. All the other variables include (LTAX) tax, (U) unemployment, (T) trade, (year) time variable, (LGDPP) GDP per capita, (LMS) money supply, (MF) monetary freedom, (D1) dummy variable, (LBB) bank branches per 100,000 adults, (D1*LBB) interaction of dummy variable with bank branches per 100,000 adults, (LBCBD) bank credit to bank deposits, and (D1*LBCBD) interaction of dummy variable with bank credit to bank deposits. For detailed descriptions, refer to section 6.3.1 and the variables summary Table A9. Standard errors are in parentheses and * $p < 0.1$, ** $p < 0.05$, *** $p < 0.01$ denote significance at 10%, 5%, and 1%, respectively.

114 *Inferences and Policy Implications*

Table A5 Interactive term of bank deposits to GDP (%)

Dependent var SE	Coef.	Corrected std. err.	T	P > |t|
L.LSE	.7881	.0619	12.72	0.000
LBD	−.1106	.0329	−3.36	0.001
D1*LBD	.0634	.0236	2.69	0.008
D1	−.0787	.0335	−2.35	0.021
LTAX	.0608	.0290	2.10	0.038
LU	−.0350	.0202	−1.73	0.086
YEAR	−.000	.0005	−1.90	0.059
LGDPP	−.1328	.0683	−1.94	0.054
LMS	−.2150	.0908	−2.37	0.020
Constant	3.144	1.161	2.71	0.008
Observations		1199		
Instruments		23		
Overall		120		
Arellano-Bond: AR(1)		0.00		
Arellano-Bond: AR(2)		0.623		
Hansen Test (p-Val)		0.491		
LBD + D1*LBD = 0				
F (1, 119) = 6.94				
Prob > F = 0.009				

The dependent variable is shadow economy (LSE). (L.LSE) is the lag of shadow economy. All the other variables include (LBD) bank deposits, (D1*LBD) interaction of dummy variable with bank deposits, (D1) dummy variable, (LTAX) tax, (U) unemployment, (year) time variable, (LGDPP) GDP per capita, and (LMS) money supply. For detailed descriptions, refer to section 6.3.1 and the variables summary Table A9.

Table A6 Interactive term of automated teller machines (ATMs)

Dependent var SE	Coef.	Corrected std. err.	Z	P > |z|
L.LSE	.9130	.1360	6.71	0.000
LATM	−.0097	.0132	−0.74	0.462
D1*LATM	−.0431	.0258	−1.67	0.095
D1	.1360	.0753	1.81	0.071
LTAX	.9792	.4940	1.98	0.047
LT	−.1127	.0367	−3.07	0.002
LGE	.3587	.1218	2.95	0.003
LMS	−.3604	.1388	−2.60	0.009
LINF	.0340	.0141	2.42	0.016
LMF	−.0409	.0754	−0.54	0.587
YEAR	−.0045	.0014	−3.17	0.002
LGDPP	−.0778	.02861	−2.72	0.007
Constant	7.988	2.273	3.51	0.000
Observations	1129			
Instruments	21			
Overall	122			

Inferences and Policy Implications   115

Dependent var SE	Coef.	Corrected std. err.	Z	P > |z|
Arellano-Bond: AR(1)	0.002			
Arellano-Bond: AR(2)	0.273			
Hansen Test (p-Val)	0.135			
LATM + D1*ATM = 0				
Chi2 (1) = 4.15				
Prob > chi2 = 0.0416				

The dependent variable is shadow economy (LSE). (L.LSE) is the lag of shadow economy. All the other variables include (LATM) automated teller machines per 100,000 adults, (D1*LATM) interaction of dummy variable with automated teller machines per 100,000 adults, (D1) dummy variable, (LTAX) tax, (LT) trade, (LGE) government expenditure, (LMS) money supply, (LINF) inflation, (LMF) monetary freedom, (year) time variable, and (LGDPP) GDP per capita. For details, refer to section 6.3.1 and the variables summary Table A9.

Table A7 Interactive term of domestic credit to private sector by banks (% of GDP)

Dependent var SE	Coef.	Corrected std. err.	t	P > |t|
L.LSE	.6173	.0749	8.25	0.000
LT	−.1035	0.037	−2.80	0.006
LGDP	−.0022	.0012	−1.76	0.081
LGE	−.0139	.0453	−0.31	0.758
LPS	−.0082	.0122	−0.67	0.501
LRQ	−.1157	.3157	−3.66	0.000
D1	.0463	.0354	1.31	0.194
LDC	−.0076	.0025	−2.99	0.003
DC_D1	−.0420	.0242	−1.73	0.085
Constant	.9977	.1626	6.13	0.000
Observations	799			
Instruments	30			
Overall	140			
Arellano-Bond: AR(1)	0.000			
Arellano-Bond: AR(2)	0.460			
Hansen Test (p-Val)	0.000			
D1*DC + LDC = 0				
F (1,139) = 4.19				
Prob > F = 0.0425				

The dependent variable is shadow economy (LSE). (L.LSE) is the lag of shadow economy. All the other variables include (LT) trade, (LGE) government expenditure, (LGDP) gross domestic product, (LPS) political stability, (RQ) regulation quality, (D1) dummy variable, (LDC) domestic credit, (DC_D1) interaction of domestic credit with dummy variable. For details, refer to section 6.3.1 and the variables summary Table A9.

116   *Inferences and Policy Implications*

Table A8 Descriptive statistics (variables in level form)[1]

Variable	Obs.	Mean	Std. dev.	Min.	Max.
SE	1,691	29.89	12.08	7.96	69.08
GDP	1,690	3.99	4.50	−36.70	38.00
MS	1,444	17.57	81.70	−54.69	3078.13
GE	1,677	15.39	4.94	2.05	31.57
GDPP	1,690	2.48	4.39	−36.83	33.03
T	1,689	91.66	56.59	21.12	442.62
TAX	1,599	0.16	0.06	0.00	0.49
U	1,680	8.23	5.51	0.10	37.60
PS	1,692	45.67	27.39	0.47	100.00
RQ	1,692	52.78	27.65	0.49	100.00
ROL	1,692	49.36	29.21	0.47	100.00
ECOF	1,682	61.28	10.08	21.40	90.10
BF	1,682	65.45	16.17	23.40	100.00
ATM	1,472	45.38	46.41	0.01	288.63
BD	1,628	51.48	51.29	2.22	479.67
BBADLT	1,611	18.06	20.39	0.12	257.70
BCBD	1,630	102.60	68.70	17.79	879.66
DCPS	1,644	55.54	48.93	0.19	312.15
MF	1,682	75.31	9.59	0.00	94.30
TF	1,682	73.60	12.19	0.00	95.00
INF	1,675	21.11	597.01	−35.84	24411.03
VA	1,692	49.53	28.70	1.88	100.00

The variables include (SE) shadow economy, (GDP) gross domestic product, money supply (MS), government expenditure (GE), GDP per capita (GDPP), trade (T), tax (TAX), unemployment (U), (PS) political stability, (RQ) regulation quality, (ROL) rule of law, (ECOF) economic freedom, (BF) business freedom, (ATM) automated teller machines per 100,000 adults, (BD) bank deposits to GDP, (BB) bank branches per 100,000 adults, (BCBD) bank credit to bank deposits, (DCPS) domestic credit to private sector, monetary freedom (MF), (TF) trade freedom, inflation (INF), and voice and accountability (VA). For details, see section 6.3.1 and the variables summary Table A9.

Table A9 List of variables

Variable[2]	Description	Expected sign	Sources
LSE	Shadow Economy (% of GDP)		
LGDP	Gross Domestic Product (Annual %)	+/-	World Development Indicators (World Bank)
LGDPP	GDP per capita growth (annual %)	-	World Development Indicators (World Bank)
LMS	Money Supply (Annual %)	+	World Development Indicators (World Bank)
LGE	Government Expenditure (% of GDP)	+/-	World Development Indicators (World Bank)
LTAX	Tax (% of GDP)	+	World Development Indicators (World Bank)

Table A9 (Continued)

Variable[2]	Description	Expected sign	Sources
LT	Trade (% of GDP)	+	World Development Indicators (World Bank)
LU	Unemployment (% of Total Labor Force)	+	World Development Indicators (World Bank)
LPS	Political Stability (Percentile Rank)	-	World Governance Indicators (World Bank)
LRQ	Regulation Quality (Percentile Rank)	-	World Governance Indicators (World Bank)
LROL	Rule of Law (Percentile Rank)	-	World Governance Indicators (World Bank)
LVA	Voice and Accountability (Percentile Rank)	-	World Governance Indicators (World Bank)
LECOF	Economic Freedom (Percentile Rank)	-	The Heritage Foundation
LTF	Trade Freedom (Percentile Rank)	-	The Heritage Foundation
LMF	Monetary Freedom (Percentile Rank)	-	The Heritage Foundation
LBF	Business Freedom (Percentile Rank)	-	The Heritage Foundation
LINF	Inflation (Annual %)	+	World Development Indicators (World Bank)
LATM	Automated Teller Machines per 100,000 adults	-	World Development Indicators (World Bank)
LBD	Bank Deposits to GDP (%)	-	World Development Indicators (World Bank)
LBB	Bank Branches per 100,000 adults	-	World Development Indicators (World Bank)
LBCBD	Bank Credit to Bank Deposits (%)	-	World Development Indicators (World Bank)
LDCPS	Domestic Credit to Private Sector (% of GDP)	-	World Development Indicators (World Bank)

118 *Inferences and Policy Implications*

Table A10 List of countries

Non-OIC countries

Angola	Czech Republic	Kenya	Rwanda
Argentina	Denmark	Korea, Rep.	Singapore
Armenia	Dominican Republic	Lao PDR	Slovak Republic
Australia	Ecuador	Latvia	Slovenia
Austria	El Salvador	Lithuania	South Africa
Bahamas	Equatorial Guinea	Luxembourg	Spain
Belarus	Estonia	Madagascar	Sri Lanka
Belgium	Fiji	Malawi	Swaziland
Belize	Finland	Malta	Sweden
Bolivia	France	Mauritius	Switzerland
Botswana	Georgia	Mexico	Tanzania
Brazil	Germany	Moldova	Thailand
Bulgaria	Ghana	Mongolia	Trinidad and Tobago
Burundi	Greece	Namibia	Ukraine
Cabo Verde	Guatemala	Nepal	United Kingdom
Cambodia	Haiti	Netherlands	United States
Canada	Honduras	New Zealand	Uruguay
Central African Republic	Hong Kong	Nicaragua	Venezuela
Chile	Hungary	Norway	Vietnam
China	Iceland	Paraguay	Zambia
Colombia	India	Peru	Zimbabwe
Congo, Dem. Rep.	Ireland	Philippines	
Congo, Rep.	Israel	Poland	
Costa Rica	Italy	Portugal	
Croatia	Jamaica	Romania	
Cyprus	Japan	Russian Federation	

OIC countries

Albania	Gabon	Lebanon	Senegal
Algeria	Gambia	Malaysia	Sierra Leone
Azerbaijan	Guinea	Mali	Suriname
Bahrain	Guinea-Bissau	Mauritania	Tajikistan
Bangladesh	Guyana	Morocco	Togo
Benin	Indonesia	Mozambique	Tunisia
Burkina Faso	Iran	Niger	Turkey
Cameroon	Jordan	Nigeria	Uganda
Chad	Kazakhstan	Oman	Yemen, Rep.
Cote d'Ivoire	Kuwait	Pakistan	
Egypt	Kyrgyzstan	Saudi Arabia	

Notes

1 We have used variables in log form where we got negative values after taking log.

2 All the variables are in natural logarithm form.

References

Abdih, M. Y., & Medina, L. (2013). *Measuring the informal economy in the Caucasus and Central Asia* (No. 13–137). International Monetary Fund, Washington, DC, 1–17.

Adam, M. C., & Ginsburgh, V. (1985). The effects of irregular markets on macroeconomic policy: Some estimates for Belgium. *European Economic Review*, *29*(1), 15–33.

Ahn, S. C., & Schmidt, P. (1995). Efficient estimation of models for dynamic panel data. *Journal of Econometrics*, *68*(1), 5–27.

Albu, L. L. (2008). A model to estimate spatial distribution of informal economy. *Journal for Economic Forecasting*, *5*(4), 111–124.

Alesina, A. (1999). Too large and too small governments. In *Economic policy & equity*, ed. Vito Tanzi, Ke-young Chu, & Sanjeev Gupta. International Monetary Fund, Washington, DC.

Anderson, T. W., & Hsiao, C. (1981). Estimation of dynamic models with error components. *Journal of the American statistical Association*, *76*(375), 598–606.

Anwar, M. (1987). *Modelling interest-free economy: A study in macroeconomics and development* (No. 4). International Institute of Islamic Thought (IIIT), Herndon, VA.

Arby, M. F., Malik, M. J., & Hanif, M. N. (2010). *The size of informal economy in Pakistan* (No 33). State Bank of Pakistan, Lahore, Pakistan.

Arellano, M., & Bond, S. (1991). Some tests of specification for panel data: Monte Carlo evidence and an application to employment equations. *The Review of Economic Studies*, *58*(2), 277–297.

Arellano, M., & Bover, O. (1995). Another look at the instrumental variable estimation of error-components models. *Journal of Econometrics*, *68*(1), 29–51.

Arias, O., & Khamis, M. (2008). *Comparative advantage, segmentation and informal earnings: A marginal treatment effects approach* (No. 3916). Institute for the Study of Labor, Bonn.

Asiedu, E., & Stengos, T. (2014). An empirical estimation of the underground economy in Ghana. *Economics Research International*, *2014*, 1–14.

Bagachwa, M. S., & Naho, A. (1995). Estimating the second economy in Tanzania. *World Development*, *23*(8), 1387–1399.

Balan, J., Browning, H. L., & Jelin, E. (1973). *Men in a developing society*, Institute of Latin American Studies, U.T. Austin. University of Texas Press, Austin, TX.

Baltagi, B. H. (2008). *Econometric analysis of panel data*. John Wiley & Sons, Hoboken, NJ.

Baltagi, B. H., Bratberg, E., & Holmås, T. H. (2005). A panel data study of physicians' labor supply: The case of Norway. *Health Economics*, *14*(10), 1035–1045.

Banerjee, B. (1983). The role of the informal sector in the migration process: A test of probabilistic migration models and labour market segmentation for India. *Oxford Economic Papers*, *35*(3), 399–422.

120   *References*

Bangasser, P. E. (2000). *The ILO and the informal sector: An institutional history*. Director, Employment Strategy, Department Employment Sector (No. 9). Geneva, Switzerland.

Barro, R. J., & Sala-i-Martin, X. (2003). *Economic growth*, volume 1 of MIT Press Books, Cambridge, MA.

Bawly, D. (1982). *The subterranean economy*. McGraw-Hill, New York.

Baxter, M. W. (1980). *Food in Fiji: The produce and processed foods distribution systems* (No. 22). Australian National University, Development Studies Centre, Canberra, Australia.

Bayar, Y., & Aytemiz, L. (2017). Financial development and shadow economy in Turkey. In *Unregistered employment*. IJOPEC Publication, London, 170.

Bayar, Y., & Ozturk, O. F. (2016). Financial development and shadow economy in European Union transition economies. *Managing Global Transitions, 14*(2), 157.

Beavon, K. S. O., & Rogerson, C. M. (1982). The informal sector of the apartheid city: The pavement people of Johannesburg. In *Living under apartheid*. Smith Publication, London.

Bechhofer, F., & Elliott, B. (Eds.). (1981). *The Petite Bourgeoisie: Comparative studies of Uneasy Stratum*. Palgrave MacMillan, London.

Beck, T., & Hoseini, M. (2014). *Informality and access to finance: Evidence from India*. Center Discussion Paper Series (No. 52). Available at https://ssrn.com/abstract=2491466 or http://doi.org/10.2139/ssrn.2491466.

Becker, G. S., Murphy, K. M., & Grossman, M. (2004). *The economic theory of illegal goods: The case of drugs* (No. 10976). Department of Economics, University of Chicago, Chicago.

Becker, K. F. (2004). *The informal sector. Stockholm: SIDA, fact finding study*. Department for Infrastructure and Economic Co-operation, Sweden.

Benería, L., Portes, A., & Castells, M. (1989). Subcontracting and employment dynamics in Mexico City. In *The informal economy: Studies in advanced and less developed countries*. Johns Hopkins University Press, Baltimore, MD.

Benton, T. (1989). Marxism and natural limits: An ecological critique and reconstruction. *New Left Review, 178*(1), 51–86.

Berdiev, A. N., & Saunoris, J. W. (2016). Financial development and the shadow economy: A panel VAR analysis. *Economic Modelling, 57*, 197–207. https://doi.org/10.1016/j.econmod.2016.03.028.

Berdiev, A. N., Saunoris, J. W., & Schneider, F. (2018). Give me liberty, or I will produce underground: Effects of economic freedom on the shadow economy. *Southern Economic Journal, 85*(2), 537–562.

Bhattacharyya, D. K. (1990). An econometric method of estimating the 'hidden economy', United Kingdom (1960–1984): Estimates and tests. *The Economic Journal, 100*(402), 703–717.

Bhattacharyya, D. K. (1993). *How does the 'hidden economy' affect consumers' expenditure? An econometric study of the UK (1960–1984)*. International Institute of Public Finance, Berlin.

Bhattacharyya, D. K. (1999). On the economic rationale of estimating the hidden economy. *The Economic Journal, 109*(456), 348–359.

Bhattacharyya, S. (2009). Root causes of African underdevelopment. *Journal of African Economies, 18*(5), 745–780.

Birkbeck, C. (1979). Garbage, industry, and the 'vultures' of Cali, Colombia. *Casual Work and Poverty in Third World Cities*, 161–183.

Bittencourt, M., Gupta, R., & Stander, L. (2014). Tax evasion, financial development and inflation: Theory and empirical evidence. *Journal of Banking & Finance, 41*, 194–208.

References 121

Blackburn, K., Bose, N., & Capasso, S. (2012). Tax evasion, the underground economy and financial development. *Journal of Economic Behavior & Organization, 83*(2), 243–253.

Blunch, N. H., Canagarajah, S., & Raju, D. (2001). The informal sector revisited: A synthesis across space and time. *World Bank Social Protection Discussion Papers, 119.*

Blundell, R., & Bond, S. (1998). Initial conditions and moment restrictions in dynamic panel data models. *Journal of Econometrics, 87*(1), 115–143.

Boeke, J. H. (1942). *Structure of Netherlands Indian economy.* Institute of Pacific Relations, New York.

Boeke, J. H. (1961). *The Theory of dualism. The concept of dualism in theory and policy.* W Van Hoeve Publisher Ltd, Amsterdam, 165–193.

Boels, D. (2014). It's better than stealing: Informal street selling in Brussels. *International Journal of Sociology and Social Policy, 34*(9/10), 670–693.

Bolnick, B. R. (1992). Moneylenders and informal financial markets in Malawi. *World Development, 20*(1), 57–68.

Bond, S. R., Hoeffler, A., & Temple, J. R. (2001). GMM estimation of empirical growth models. *Discussion Paper* (No. 2048). Centre for Economic Policy Research.

Bond, S. R., & Windmeijer, F. (2002). *Finite sample inference for GMM estimators in linear panel data models* (No. 04/02). A Comparison of Alternative Tests. Mimeo, Institute for Fiscal Studies, London.

Bose, N., Capasso, S., & Andreas Wurm, M. (2012). The impact of banking development on the size of shadow economies. *Journal of Economic Studies, 39*(6), 620–638.

Bourhaba, O., & Mama, H. (2016). An estimation of the informal economy in Morocco. *International Journal of Economics and Finance, 8*(9), 140.

Bovi, M., & Dell'Anno, R. (2010). The changing nature of the OECD shadow economy. *Journal of Evolutionary Economics, 20*(1), 20.

Bromley, R. (1978). Introduction: The urban informal sector: Why is it worth discussing? *World Development, 6*(9/10), 1033–1039.

Bromley, R., & Gerry, C. (Eds.). (1979). *Casual work and poverty in third world cities.* Wiley, Chichester.

Brown, D., & McGranahan, G. (2016). The urban informal economy, local inclusion and achieving a global green transformation. *Habitat International, 53*, 97–105.

Cagan, P. (1958). The demand for currency relative to the total money supply. *Journal of Political Economy, 66*(4), 303–328.

Capasso, S., & Jappelli, T. (2013). Financial development and the underground economy. *Journal of Development Economics, 101*, 167–178.

Carter, M. (1984). Issues in the hidden economy – a survey. *Economic Record, 60*(3), 209–221.

Castells, M., & Portes, A. (1989). World underneath: The origins, dynamics, and effects of the informal economy. In *The informal economy: Studies in advanced and less developed countries*, ed. Alejandro Portes, Manuel Castells, & Lauren A. Benton. Johns Hopkins University Press, Baltimore, 12.

Cebula, R. J. (1997). An empirical analysis of the impact of government tax and auditing policies on the size of the underground economy. *American Journal of Economics and Sociology, 56*(2), 173–185.

Chandavarkar, A. (1988). The informal sector: Empty box or portmanteau concept?: (A comment). *World Development, 16*(10), 1259–1261.

Charmes, J. (2014). Informality after 40 years of debates: Origins, development and ambiguities of a successful concept. *World Development, 2014.*

122 References

Chaudhuri, K., Schneider, F., & Chattopadhyay, S. (2006). The size and development of the shadow economy: An empirical investigation from states of India. *Journal of Development Economics, 80*(2), 428–443.

Chaudhuri, T. D. (1989). A theoretical analysis of the informal sector. *World Development, 17*(3), 351–355.

Chen, M. A. (2005). Rethinking the informal economy: From enterprise characteristics to employment relations. *In Rethinking Informalization, 28*.

Chen, M. A. (2012). The informal economy: Definitions, theories and policies. *Women in informal economy globalizing and organizing: WIEGO working paper, 1* (No. 26, 90141–90144). WIEGO, Cambridge/Manchester.

Chen, M. A., Jhabvala, R., & Lund, F. (2002). *Supporting workers in the informal economy: A policy framework*. International Labour Office, Geneva.

Chen, M. A., Vanek, J., & Carr, M. (2004). *Mainstreaming informal employment and gender in poverty reduction: A handbook for policy-makers and other stakeholders*. Commonwealth Secretariat, and the International Development research Centre, London and Ottawa.

Chengelova, E. (2016). Holistic approach for studying the shadow economy: The case of bulgaria. *Экономическая социология, 17*(5), 159.

Choi, J. P., & Thum, M. (2005). Corruption and the shadow economy. *International Economic Review, 46*(3), 817–836.

Contini, B. (1983). The second economy in Italy. In *The underground economy in the United States and Abroad*. DC Heath, Boston, 1982, 199–208.

Cumming, D. J., Leboef, G., & Schwienbacher, A. (2014). Crowdfunding models: Keep-it-all versus all-or-nothing. *Working Paper*. York University and University of Lille.

Dabla-Norris, E., Gradstein, M., & Inchauste, G. (2008). What causes firms to hide output? The determinants of informality. *Journal of Development Economics, 85*(1), 1–27.

Dannhaeuser, N. (1977). Distribution and the structure of retail trade in a Philippine commercial town setting. *Economic Development and Cultural Change, 25*(3), 471–503.

Dasgupta, S. (2003). Structural and behavioural characteristics of informal service employment: Evidence from a survey in New Delhi. *Journal of Development Studies, 39*(3), 51–80.

Debrah, Y. A. (2007). Promoting the informal sector as a source of gainful employment in developing countries: Insights from Ghana. *The International Journal of Human Resource Management, 18*(6), 1063–1084.

De Koker, L., & Jentzsch, N. (2013). Financial inclusion and financial integrity: Aligned incentives? *World Development, 44*, 267–280.

Del Boca, D., & Forte, F. (1982). Recent empirical surveys and theoretical interpretations of the parallel economy in Italy. In *The underground economy in the United States and Abroad*. Lexington Books, MA, 160–178.

Dell'Anno, R. (2003). *Estimating the shadow economy in Italy: A structural equation approach* (No. 7). Department of Economics and Statistics, University of Salerno.

Dell'Anno, R. (2007). The shadow economy in Portugal: An analysis with the MIMIC approach. *Journal of Applied Economics, 10*(2), 253.

Dell'Anno, R., Davidescu, A. A., & Balele, N. W. P. (2018). Estimating shadow economy in Tanzania: An analysis with the MIMIC approach. *Journal of Economic Studies, 45*(1), 100–113.

Dell'Anno, R., Gómez-Gómez, M., & Pardo, Á. A. (2004). *Shadow economy in three very different Mediterranean countries: France, Spain and Greece*. A MIMIC approach.

Dell'Anno, R., Gómez-Antonio, M., & Pardo, Á. A. (2007). The shadow economy in three Mediterranean countries: France, Spain and Greece. A MIMIC approach. *Empirical Economics, 33*(1), 51–84. https://doi.org/10.1007/s00181-006-0084-3

References 123

Dell'Anno, R., & Schneider, F. (2003). The shadow economy of Italy and other OECD countries: What do we know? *Journal of Public Finance and Public Choice, 21*(2–3), 97–120.

De Soto, H. (1989). *The other path.* New York: Harper & Row, 255.

Din, B. H., Habibullah, M. S., Baharom, A. H., & Saari, M. D. (2016). Are shadow economy and tourism related? International evidence. *Procedia Economics and Finance, 35,* 173–178.

Djankov, S., La Porta, R., Lopez-de-Silanes, F., & Shleifer, A. (2002). The regulation of entry. *The Quarterly Journal of Economics, 117*(1), 1–37.

Dotti, N. F., Van Heur, B., & Williams, C. C. (2015). Mapping the shadow economy: Spatial variations in the use of high denomination bank notes in Brussels. *European Spatial Research and Policy, 22*(1), 5–21.

Dreher, A., Kotsogiannis, C., & McCorriston, S. (2009). How do institutions affect corruption and the shadow economy? *International Tax and Public Finance, 16*(6), 773.

Du Toit, A., & Hickey, S. (2007). *Adverse incorporation, social exclusion and chronic poverty.* CPRC working paper 81. University of Manchester and PLAAS, Manchester & Bellville.

Economics focus: In the shadows. *The Economist,* 2015, March 4. Available at https://www.economist.com/finance-and-economics/2004/06/17/in-the-shadows

Eilat, Y., & Zinnes, C. (2000). The evolution of the shadow economy in transition countries: Consequences for economic growth and donor assistance. *Harvard institute for international development, CAER II discussion paper, 83.* Harvard Institute for International Development. Cambridge, MA.

Eilat, Y., & Zinnes, C. (2002). The shadow economy in transition countries: Friend or foe? A policy perspective. *World Development, 30*(7), 1233–1254.

Ela, M. (2013). An assessment on the relationship between informal economy and educational level in Turkey. *International Journal of Economics and Financial Issues, 3*(4), 910.

Elbahnasawy, N. G., Ellis, M. A., & Adom, A. D. (2016). Political instability and the informal economy. *World Development, 85,* 31–42.

Elgin, C., & Uras, B. R. (2013). Is informality a barrier to financial development? *SERIEs, 4*(3), 309–331.

Encyclopedia. (2005). *Collins discovery encyclopedia* (1st ed.). HarperCollins Publishers, Glasgow, Scotland.

Erdinç, Z. (2012). Currency demand modeling in estimating the underground economy in Turkey: An error correction framework. *International Research Journal of Finance and Economic, 96,* 15–27.

Farazi, S. (2014). Informal firms and financial inclusion: status and determinants. *Journal of International Commerce, Economics and Policy, 5*(3).

Fedotenkov, I., & Schneider, F. (2017). *Military expenditures and shadow economy in the Baltic States: Is there a link?* https://mpra.ub.uni-muenchen.de/76194/. Accessed 18 April 2020.

Feige, E. L. (1979). How big is the irregular economy? *Challenge, 22*(5), 5–13.

Feige, E. L. (1989). *The underground economies: Tax evasion and information distortion.* Cambridge University Press, Cambridge.

Feige, E. L. (2003). Dynamics of currency substitution, asset substitution and de facto dollarization and euroization in transition countries. *Comparative Economic Studies, 45*(3), 358–383.

Feige, E. L. (2007). *The underground economies: Tax evasion and information distortion.* Cambridge University Press, Cambridge.

Feld, L. P., & Schneider, F. (2010). Survey on the shadow economy and undeclared earnings in OECD countries. *German Economic Review, 11*(2), 109–149.

124   *References*

Fernández-Kelly, M. P., & Garcia, A. M. (1989). Informalization at the core: Hispanic women, homework, and the advanced capitalist state. *The Informal Economy: Studies in Advanced and Less Developed Countries*, 247–264.

Forbes, D. K. (1981). *Development and the' informal 'sector: A study of Peddlars and Trishaw Riders in Ujung Pandang, Indonesia* (Doctoral dissertation). Monash University.

Franzoni, L. A. (1998). Independent auditors as fiscal gatekeepers. *International Review of Law and Economics*, *18*(4), 365–384.

Frey, B. S., & Schneider, F. (2000). Informal and underground economy (No. 0004). *Working paper*, Department of Economics, Johannes Kepler University of Linz.

Frey, B. S., & Weck-Hanneman, H. (1984). The hidden economy as an 'unobserved' variable. *European Economic Review*, *26*(1–2), 33–53.

Friedman, E., Johnson, S., Kaufmann, D., & Zoido-Lobaton, P. (2000). Dodging the grabbing hand: The determinants of unofficial activity in 69 countries. *Journal of Public Economics*, *76*(3), 459–493.

Friedman, M. (1947, June 8). NBC radio Personal interview.

Fuest, C., & Riedel, N. (2009). Tax evasion, tax avoidance and tax expenditures in developing countries: A review of the literature. *Report prepared for the UK Department for International Development (DFID)*. Oxford University Centre for Business Taxation, Said Business School, Park End Street, Oxford, OX1 1 HP, 1–69.

Furnivall, J. S. (1939). *Netherlands India: A study of political economy*. Cambridge University Press, Cambridge.

Gatti, R., & Honorati, M. (2008). Informality among formal firms: Firm-level. 'Cross-country evidence on tax compliance and access to credit' World Bank. *Policy Research Paper*, *4476*.

Geertz, C. (1963). *Peddlers and princes: Social development and economic change in two Indonesian towns* (Vol. 318). University of Chicago Press, Chicago.

Geertz, C. (1978). The bazaar economy: Information and search in peasant marketing: Papers and proceedings of the ninetieth annual meeting of the American economic association. *The American Economic Review*, *68*(2), 28–32.

Gerry, C., & Birkbeck, C. (1981). The petty commodity producer in third world cities: Petit-bourgeois or 'disguised' proletarian? In *The petite bourgeoisie*. Palgrave Macmillan, London, 121–154.

Gërxhani, K. (2004). The informal sector in developed and less developed countries: A literature survey. *Public Choice*, *120*(3–4), 267–300.

Giles, D. E. (1999a). Measuring the hidden economy: Implications for econometric modelling. *The Economic Journal*, *109*(456), 370–380.

Giles, D. E., & Johnson, B. J. (2000). *Taxes, risk-aversion, and the size of the underground economy: A nonparametric analysis with New Zealand data*. Department of Economics, University of Victoria, BC.

Giles, D. E., & Tedds, L. M. (2002). *Taxes and the Canadian underground economy*. Canadian Tax Paper 106. Canadian Tax Foundation, Toronto.

Gobbi, G., & Zizza, R. (2007). *Does the underground economy hold back financial deepening? Evidence from the Italian credit market. Evidence from the Italian Credit Market (November 2007). Working Paper* (No. 646). Bank of Italy, Temi di discussione.

González-Fernández, M., & González-Velasco, C. (2015). Analysis of the shadow economy in the Spanish regions. *Journal of Policy Modeling*, *37*(6), 1049–1064.

Guibourg, G., & Segendorf, B. L. (2007). *The use of cash and the size of the shadow economy in Sweden*. Riksbank research paper series (No. 204). Available at SSRN: https://ssrn.com/abstract=1022024 or http://dx.doi.org/10.2139/ssrn.1022024.

References   125

Gulzar, A., Junaid, N., & Haider, A. (2010). What is hidden, in the hidden economy of Pakistan? Size, causes, issues, and implications. *The Pakistan Development Review*, 665–704.

Hall, I. (2017). The age of aspiration: Power, wealth, and conflict in globalizing India, Why India is not a Great Power (*yet*). *International Affairs*, *93*(1), 229–231.

Hart, K. (1970). 8. Small-scale entrepreneurs in Ghana and development planning. *The Journal of Development Studies*, *6*(4), 104–120.

Hart, K. (1971). Migration and tribal identity among the Frafras of Ghana. *Journal of Asian and African Studies*, *6*(1), 21–36.

Hart, K. (1973). Informal income opportunities and urban employment in Ghana. *The Journal of Modern African Studies*, *11*(1), 61–89.

Hart, K. (2012, October 17). *How the informal economy took over the world*, at 6:30pm. Available at http://openanthcoop.ning.com/profiles/blogs/the-informalization-of-the-world-economy#sthash.WgShns3n.dpbs.

Hassan, M., & Schneider, F. (2016). Modelling the Egyptian shadow economy: A MIMIC model and a currency demand approach. *Journal of Economics and Political Economy*, *3*(2), 309.

Helberger, C., & Knepel, H. (1988). How big is the shadow economy?: A re-analysis of the unobserved-variable approach of BS Frey and H. Weck-Hannemann. *European Economic Review*, *32*(4), 965–976.

Hemmer, H. R., & Mannel, C. (1989). On the economic analysis of the urban informal sector. *World Development*, *17*(10), 1543–1552.

Hill, R., & Kabir, M. (1996). Tax rates, the tax mix, and the growth of the underground economy in Canada: What can we infer. *Canadian Tax Journal/Revue Fiscale Canadienne*, *44*(6), 1552–1583.

Hosseini, A., Nasrollahi, Z., & Abtahi, S. Y. (2014). Estimation of underground economy in Iran and its relationship with financial development: application ARDL. *Journal of Novel Applied sciences, 2015 JNAS Journal. 2014-4-3*, 360–370.

Hussmanns, R. (2004). *Measuring the informal economy: From employment in the informal sector to informal employment*. Working paper (No. 53). Policy Integration Department, Bureau of Statistics, International labour Office.

ICMIF. (2010). *Global mutual market share*. International Cooperative and Mutual Insurance Federation.

ICMIF. (2015). *Mutual microinsurance strategy: Building resilience in vulnerable communities*. Bay, Laguna. Available at https://www.icmif.org/5-5-5-introduction.

IFC (International Finance Corporation). 2012. *Enterprise finance gap database*. World Bank, Washington, DC.

IFC (International Finance Corporation). 2014. *Islamic banking opportunities across small and medium enterprises in MENA*. World Bank, Washington, DC.

Igudia, E. O. (2014). *The Nigerian informal economy: A regional analysis* (Doctoral Dissertation). Nottingham Trent University.

Ihrig, J., & Moe, K. S. (2004). Lurking in the shadows: The informal sector and government policy. *Journal of Development Economics*, *73*(2), 541–557.

ILO (International Labor Organization). (1972). *Employment, incomes and equity: A strategy for increasing productivity in Kenya*. ILO, Geneva.

ILO (International Labor Organization). (1993). *Statistics of employment in the informal sector*. XVI Conference of Labor Statisticians, Geneva, Report III.

ILO (International Labor Organization). (2002). *Decent work and the informal economy*. Report of the Director-General presented to the 90th International Labour Conference. International Labour Office, Geneva.

126   References

ILO (International Labor Organization). (2013a). *Measuring informality: A statistical manual on the informal sector and informal employment*. International Labour Organization, Geneva.

ILO (International Labor Organization). (2013b). *Measuring the size of the informal sector*. ILO informal Sector Web Site. Available at http://lnweb90.worldbank.org/eca/eca.nsf/OpenDocument.

ILO & WTO. (2009). *Globalization and informal jobs in developing countries*. Geneva.

Imamoglu, H. (2017). Estimating the roles of financial sector development and international trade openness in underground economies: Evidence from the European Union. Economics Discussion Papers (No. 2017–50). Kiel Institute for the World Economy (IfW Kiel). Available at https://ideas.repec.org/p/zbw/ifwedp/201750.html

Jagannathan, N. V. (1987). *Informal markets in developing countries*. Oxford University Press, Oxford.

Jellinek, L. (1978). Circular migration and the Pondok dwelling pattern: A case study of ice-cream traders in Jarkarta. In *Food shelter and transport in South East Asia and the pacific*, ed. P. Rimmer, D. W. Drakakis-Smith, & T. G. McGee. Australian National University, Canberra, 135–154.

Johnson, S., Kaufmann, D., McMillan, J., & Woodruff, C. (2000). Why do firms hide? Bribes and unofficial activity after communism. *Journal of Public Economics, 76*(3), 495–520.

Johnson, S., Kaufmann, D., Shleifer, A., Goldman, M. I., & Weitzman, M. L. (1997). The unofficial economy in transition. *Brookings Papers on Economic Activity, 1997*(2), 159–239.

Johnson, S., Kaufmann, D., & Zoido-Lobaton, P. (1998a). Regulatory discretion and the unofficial economy. *The American Economic Review, 88*(2), 387–392.

Johnson, S., Kaufmann, D., & Zoido-Lobaton, P. (1998b). *Corruption, public finances and the unofficial economy*. The World Bank, Washington, DC, Discussion Paper.

Joo, D. (2011). Determinants of the informal sector and their effects on the economy: The case of Korea. *Global Economic Review, 40*(1), 21–43.

Kabbara, A. H. S. (2014). *The foundations of Islamic economics and banking*. Partridge, Singapore.

Kamali, M. H. (2005). *Principles of Islamic jurisprudence*. IB Tauris, Islamic Texts Society, Cambridge, UK, 165.

Kaplinsky, R. (1979). Export-oriented growth: A large international firm in a small developing country. *World Development, 7*(8–9), 825–834.

Karlinger, L. (2009). The underground economy in the late 1990s: Evading taxes, or evading competition? *World Development, 37*(10), 1600–1611.

Kaufmann, D., & Kaliberda, A. (1996). Integrating the unofficial economy into the dynamics of post-socialist economies. In *Economic transition in the newly independent states*, ed. B. Kaminsky. M.E. Sharpe Press, Armonk, NY.

Kaur, S. (2016). Demonetization and its impacts in India. *International Journal of Research, 3*(17), 1150–1154.

Kesteltoot, C., & Meert, H. (1999). Informal spaces: The geography of informal economic activities in Brussels. *International Journal of Urban and Regional Research, 23*(2), 232–251.

Khundker, N. (1988). The fuzziness of the informal sector: Can we afford to throw out the baby with the bath water?: (A comment). *World Development, 16*(10), 1263–1265.

Kim, D. W., Yu, J. S., & Hassan, M. K. (2018). Financial inclusion and economic growth in OIC countries. *Research in International Business and Finance, 43*, 1–14.

References 127

King, K. J. (1974). Kenya's informal machine-makers: A study of small-scale industry in Kenya's emergent artisan society. *World Development*, 2(4), 9–28.

Kirchgaessner, G. (1983). Size and development of the West German shadow economy, 1955–1980. *Zeitschrift Für Die Gesamte Staatswissenschaft/Journal of Institutional and Theoretical Economics*, 197–214.

Klovland, J. T. (1984). Tax evasion and the demand for currency in Norway and Sweden. Is there a hidden relationship? *The Scandinavian Journal of Economics*, 423–439.

Langdon, S. (1975). Multinational corporations, taste transfer and underdevelopment: A case study from Kenya. *Review of African Political Economy*, 2(2), 12–35.

Law, S. H., & Singh, N. (2014). Does too much finance harm economic growth? *Journal of Banking & Finance*, 41, 36–44.

Lemieux, T., Fortin, B., & Frechette, P. (1994). The effect of taxes on labor supply in the underground economy. *The American Economic Review*, 231–254.

Leonard, M. (1994). *Informal economic activity in Belfast*. Avebury, Aldershot.

Leonard, M. (1998). *Invisible work, invisible workers: The informal economy in Europe and the US*. Macmillan, London.

Levenson, A. R., & Maloney, W. F. (1998). *The informal sector, firm dynamics and institutional participation*. IBRD working paper 1988. Latin America and the Caribbean Region, Poverty Reduction and Economic Management Unit, World Bank, Washington, DC.

Lewis, W. A. (1954). Economic development with unlimited supplies of labour. *The Manchester School*, 22(2), 139–191.

Lewis, W. A. (1955). Arthur: The theory of economic growth. *Homewood*, 111, 9.

Likic-Brboric, B., Slavnic, Z., & Woolfson, C. (2013). Labour migration and informalisation: East meets West. *International Journal of Sociology and Social Policy*, 33(11/12), 677–692.

Lindell, I. (2010). Between exit and voice: Informality and the spaces of popular agency 1. *African Studies Quarterly*, 11(2/3), 1.

Lozano, B. (1989). *The invisible workforce: Transforming American business with outside and home-based workers*. Free Press, New York.

Lucas Jr, R. E. (1978). On the size distribution of business firms. *The Bell Journal of Economics*, 508–523.

Lucinda, C., & Arvate, P. (2005). A study on the shadow economy and the tax-gap: The case of CPMF in Brazil. *The Public Choice Society*, 10–13.

Mahmoudzadeh, M., Sadeghi, S., & Sadeghi, S. (2017). Fiscal spending and crowding out effect: A comparison between developed and developing countries. *Institutions and Economies*, 31–40.

Maki, D. (2012). Tests for cointegration allowing for an unknown number of breaks. *Economic Modelling*, 29(5), 2011–2015.

Malek, N. A., & Arshad, M. N. M. (2017). The informal economy: A neglected area in Islamic economics. *International Journal of Economics, Management and Accounting*, 25(2), 285.

Maloney, W. F. (2004). Informality revisited. *World Development*, 32(7), 1159–1178.

Mankiw, N. G., Romer, D., & Weil, D. N. (1992). A contribution to the empirics of economic growth. *The Quarterly Journal of Economics*, 107(2), 407–437.

Marinov, A. (2008). Hidden economy in the rural regions of Bulgaria. *International Review on Public and Nonprofit Marketing*, 5(1), 71–80.

Mazumdar, D. (1976). The urban informal sector. *World Development*, 4(8), 655–679.

McGee, T. G., Ward, R. G., & Drakakis-Smith, D. W. (1980). *Food distribution in the new hebrides*. Monograph No. 28. Development Studies Centre, ANU, Canberra.

128   *References*

Meagher, K. (1995). Crisis, informalization and the urban informal sector in sub-Saharan Africa. *Development and Change, 26*(2), 259–284.

Meagher, K. (2013). *Unlocking the informal economy: A literature review on linkages between formal and informal economies in developing countries* (No. 27). Women in Informal Employment: Globalizing and Organizing (WIEGO), Cambridge.

Medina, L., & Schneider, F. (2017). *Shadow economies around the world: New results for 158 countries over 1991–2015*. CESifo Working Paper (No. 6430). Available at SSRN: https://ssrn.com/abstract=2965972.

Merrick, T. W. (1976). Employment and earnings in the informal sector in Brazil: The case of Belo Horizonte. *The Journal of Developing Areas, 10*(3), 337–354.

Mitlin, D., & Satterthwaite, D. (2013). *Urban poverty in the global south: Scale and nature*. Routledge, Abingdon & New York.

Mohieldin, M., Iqbal, Z., Rostom, A., & Fu, X. (2011). The role of Islamic finance in enhancing financial inclusion in Organisation of Islamic Cooperation (OIC) countries. *8th international conference on Islamic economics and finance on sustainable growth and inclusive economic development from an islamic perspective*. Qatar National Convention Center, Doha.

Moser, C. O. (1978). Informal sector or petty commodity production: Dualism or dependence in urban development? *World Development, 6*(9–10), 1041–1064.

Mummert, A., & Schneider, F. (2002). The German shadow economy: Parted in a united Germany? *Finanzarchiv: Public Finance Analysis, 58*(3), 286–316.

Mushtaq, S. (2017). Islamic banking: Concept and future potential in India. *International Journal of Emerging Trends in Science and Technology, 8*(4), 5465–6473.

Naidoo, G. P. (2002). *An investigation into linkages between the formal and informal sectors in South Africa using the 1993 input-output table (1993)*. Vista University, Pretoria.

Nastav, B., & Bojnec, Š. (2008). Small businesses and the shadow economy. *Czech Journal of Economics and Finance (Finance a uver), 58*(01–02), 68–81.

Nattrass, N. J. (1987). Street trading in Transkei – A struggle against poverty, persecution, and prosecution. *World Development, 15*(7), 861–875.

Nchor, D., & Adamec, V. (2015). Unofficial economy estimation by the MIMIC model: The case of Kenya, Namibia, Ghana and Nigeria. *Acta Universitatis Agriculturae et Silviculturae Mendelianae Brunensis, 63*, 222.

Nchor, D., Adamec, V., & Kolman, P. (2016). Comparison of shadow economies: The case of Ghana, Nigeria and UK. *Mediterranean Journal of Social Sciences, 7*(1), 248.

Neaime, S., & Gaysset, I. (2017). Sustainability of macroeconomic policies in selected MENA countries: Post financial and debt crises. *Research in International Business and Finance, 40*, 129–140.

Neuwirth, R. (2011, October). The Shadow Superpower. *Foreign Policy*. Available at https://foreignpolicy.com/.

Nihan, G., Demol, E., & Jondoh, C. (1979). The modern informal sector in Lomé. *International Labour Review, 118*, 631.

Nihan, G., & Jourdain, R. (1978). The modern informal sector in Nouakchott. *International Labour Review, 117*, 709.

Nikoopour, H. (2005). Measuring the size of underground economy in Iran with emphasis on the incentives for evasion of insurance premium payment (1961–2001). *Tamin-e Ejtemaie Social Security Quarterly, 6*(18).

Nikopour, H., & Habibullah, M. S. (2010). *Shadow economy and poverty*. Working Paper, MPRA Munich Personal RePEc Archive, Paper No. 23599. http://mpra.ub.uni-muenchen.de/23599/1/MPRA_paper_23599.pdf.

References 129

Ninsin, K. A. (1991). *The informal sector in Ghana's political economy*. Freedom Publications, Accra.

Norcliffe, G. (1983). Operating characteristics of rural non-farm enterprises in Central Province, Kenya. *World Development, 11*(11), 981–994.

O'Conner, A. (1983). *The African city*. Holmes and Meier Publishers, New York.

Öğünç, F., & Yılmaz, G. (2000). Estimating the underground economy in Turkey. *CBRT Research Department Discussion Paper, 15*.

Onnis, L., & Tirelli, P. (2011). *Institutions, policies and economic development. What are the causes of the shadow economy?* (No. 206). Department of Economics, University of Milan - Bicocca, Italy, available at: https://ideas.repec.org/p/mib/wpaper/206.html.

Organisation for Economic Co-operation and Development. (2009). *Competition policy and the informal economy: A handbook*. Organisation for Economic Co-operation and Development, Paris, 1–269. Available at https://www.oecd.org/daf/competition/44547855.pdf.

Organisation of Islamic Cooperation. (2016). *7th meeting of the COMCEC poverty alleviation working group*. Ankara, Turkey.

Orviská, M., Čaplánová, A., Medved, J., & Hudson, J. (2006). A cross-section approach to measuring the shadow economy. *Journal of Policy Modeling, 28*(7), 713–724.

Ott, K. (1998). Economic policy and unofficial economy in transition: the case of Croatia. In *Paper for the international conference to be held in Bled, Slovenia in September*. Institute of Public Finance, Bled, Slovenia.

Ott, K. (2002). The underground economy in Croatia. *Occasional Paper Series-Institute of Public Finance, 7*(12), 1–29.

Ouédraogo, I. M. (2017). Governance, corruption, and the informal economy. *Modern Economy, 8*(02), 256.

Papyrakis, E. (2014). A development curse: Formal vs informal activities in resource-dependent economies. *International Journal of Social Economics, 41*(3), 244–264.

Peattie, L. R. (1982). What is to be done with the 'informal sector'?: A case study of shoe manufacturers in Colombia. In *Towards a political economy of urbanization in third world countries*. Oxford University Press, Delhi.

Pedersen, S. (2003). *The shadow economy in Germany, Great Britain and Scandinavia: A measurement based on questionnaire surveys* (No. 10). Rockwool Foundation Research Unit, Copenhagen.

Pissarides, C. A., & Weber, G. (1989). An expenditure-based estimate of Britain's black economy. *Journal of Public Economics, 39*(1), 17–32.

Porta, R. L., & Shleifer, A. (2008). *The unofficial economy and economic development* (No. w14520). National Bureau of Economic Research. Brookings Papers on Economic Activity, Fall.

Portes, A. (1994). When more can be less: Labor standards, development, and the informal economy. *Contrapunto: The Informal Sector Debate in Latin America*, 113–129.

Portes, A., Castells, M., & Benton, L. A. (Eds.). (1989). *The informal economy: Studies in advanced and less developed countries*. Johns Hopkins University Press, Baltimore.

Portes, A., & Sassen-Koob, S. (1987). Making it underground: Comparative material on the informal sector in Western market economies. *American journal of Sociology, 93*(1), 30–61.

Potts, D. (2008). The urban informal sector in sub-Saharan Africa: From bad to good (and back again?). *Development Southern Africa, 25*(2), 151–167.

Public Broadcasting Service (PBS). (2000, January 10). *Interview with Milton Friedman*. Available at www.pbs.org/wgbh/commandingheights/shared/minitext/int_miltonfriedman.html#2.

Putniņš, T. J., & Sauka, A. (2015). Measuring the shadow economy using company managers. *Journal of Comparative Economics, 43*(2), 471–490.

130 References

Ranieri, R., & Almeida Ramos, R. (2013). *Inclusive growth: Building up a concept.* Working Paper (No. 104). International Policy Centre for Inclusive Growth, Brasilia.

Razmi, S. M. J., Falahi, M. A., & Montazeri, S. (2013). Institutional quality and underground economy of 51 OIC member countries. *Universal Journal of Management and Social Sciences, 3.*

Remeikiene, R. I. T. A., & Gaspareniene, L. I. G. I. T. A. (2015). Evaluation of the shadow economy influencing factors: Lithuanian case. In *9th international conference on business administration.* United Arab Emirates, Dubai.

Reuters, T., & Standard, D. (2016). *State of the Global Islamic Economy 2017/18 (SGIE).* Thomson Reuters, Dubai.

Risteski, H. (2016). Assessing handicraft shadow economy in Macedonia. *CEA Journal of Economics, 4*(1).

Roodman, D. (2006). *How to Do Xtabond2: An Introduction to Difference and System GMM in Stata* (No. 103). Center for Global Development.

Roodman, D. (2009). How to do xtabond2: An introduction to difference and system GMM in Stata. *The Stata Journal, 9*(1), 86–136.

Rosen, S. (1982). Authority, control, and the distribution of earnings. *The Bell Journal of Economics, 13*(Autumn), 311–323.

Rothenberg, A. D., Gaduh, A., Burger, N. E., Chazali, C., Tjandraningsih, I., Radikun, R., . . . & Weilant, S. (2016). Rethinking Indonesia's informal sector. *World Development, 80,* 96–113.

Roy, A. (2005). Urban informality: Toward an epistemology of planning. *Journal of the American Planning Association, 71*(2), 147–158.

Sadr, M. B. (1982). *Our economics* (English Translation). World Organization for Islamic Services, Tehran.

Santos, M. (1977). Spatial dialectics: The two circuits of urban economy in underdeveloped countries. *Antipode, 9*(3), 49–60.

Saraç, M., & Başar, R. (2014). The effect of informal economy on the European debt crisis. *Siyaset, Ekonomi ve Yönetim Araştırmaları Dergisi, 2*(2), 25–37.

Sarafidis, V., Yamagata, T., & Robertson, D. (2009). A test of cross section dependence for a linear dynamic panel model with regressors. *Journal of Econometrics, 148*(2), 149–161.

Sargan, J. D. (1975). *A suggested technique for computing approximations to Wald criteria with application to testing dynamic specifications* (No. 2). London School of Economics, London.

Sassen, S. (1994). The informal economy: Between new developments and old regulations. *Yale Law Journal, 103*(8), 2289–2304.

Sassen-Koob, S. (1989). New York City's informal economy. In *The informal economy: Studies in advanced and less developed countries.* Informal Economy, New York.

Schaefer, K. K. (2002). *Macroeconomic implications of an urban informal sector: A theoretical model and a South African case study* (Doctoral thesis). Faculty of Arts and Sciences, American University. Washington, DC.

Schneider, F. (1986). Estimating the size of the Danish shadow economy using the currency demand approach: An attempt. *The Scandinavian Journal of Economics, 88*(4), 643–668.

Schneider, F. (1994a). Measuring the size and development of the shadow economy. Can the causes be found and the obstacles be overcome? In *Essays on economic psychology.* Springer, Berlin, Heidelberg, 193–212.

Schneider, F. (1994b). Can the informal economy be reduced through major tax reforms? An empirical investigation for Austria. *Supplement to Public Finance/Finances Publius, 49,* 137–152.

References   131

Schneider, F. (1997). The informal economies of Western Europe. *Journal of the Institute of Economic Affairs*, *17*(3), 42–48.

Schneider, F. (1998a). *Further empirical results of the size of the informal economy of 17 OECD-countries over time*. Paper to be presented at the 54. Congress of the IIPF Cordowa. University of Linz, Linz, Austria.

Schneider, F. (2000). *The increase of the size of the informal economy of 18 OECD countries: some preliminary explanations*. Paper presented at the annual public choice meeting, Charleston.

Schneider, F. (2002). *Size and measurement of the informal economy in 110 countries*. Paper presented at the Workshop of Australian National Tax Centre, ANU, Canberra.

Schneider, F. (2003). *The size and development of the shadow economy around the world and relation to the hard-to-tax* (No. 0324). International Center for Public Policy, Andrew Young School of Policy Studies, Georgia State University.

Schneider, F. (2005). Shadow economies around the world: What do we really know? *European Journal of Political Economy*, *21*(3), 598–642.

Schneider, F. (2007). Does the shadow economy pose a challenge to economic and public finance policy?-Some preliminary findings. In *Public economics and public choice*. Springer, Berlin, Heidelberg, 157–180.

Schneider, F. (2008). Shadow economy. In *Readings in public choice and constitutional political economy*. Springer, Boston, MA, 511–532.

Schneider, F. (2010). The influence of public institutions on the shadow economy: An empirical investigation for OECD countries. *Review of Law & Economics*, *6*(3), 441–468.

Schneider, F. (Ed.). (2011). *Handbook on the shadow economy*. Edward Elgar Publishing, Cheltenham.

Schneider, F., Buehn, A., & Montenegro, C. E. (2010). New estimates for the shadow economies all over the world. *International Economic Journal*, *24*(4), 443–461.

Schneider, F., Buehn, A., & Montenegro, C. E. (2011). Shadow economies all over the world: New estimates for 162 countries from 1999 to 2007. In *Handbook on the shadow economy*. Edward Elgar Publishing, Cheltenham.

Schneider, F., Chaudhuri, K., & Chatterjee, S. (2003). *The size and development of the Indian shadow economy and a comparison with other 18 Asian countries: An empirical investigation* (No. 0302). Department of Economics, Johannes Kepler University of Linz, Austria.

Schneider, F., & Enste, D. H. (2000). Shadow economies: Size, causes, and consequences. *Journal of Economic Literature*, *38*(1), 77–114.

Schneider, F., & Enste, D. H. (2013). *The shadow economy: An international survey*. Cambridge University Press, Cambridge.

Schneider, F., & Hametner, B. (2014). The shadow economy in Colombia: Size and effects on economic growth. *Peace Economics, Peace Science and Public Policy*, *20*(2), 293–325.

Schneider, F., & Klinglmair, R. (2004). *Shadow economies around the world: What do we know?* (No. 1167). CESifo. Available at SSRN: https://ssrn.com/abstract=518526.

Schneider, F., & Williams, C. C. (2013). *The shadow economy*. The Institute of Economic Affairs, London. Available at https://works.bepress.com/colin_williams/23/.

Schneider, M. F., & Enste, D. (2002). *Hiding in the shadows: The growth of the underground economy*. International Monetary Fund, Washington.

Sethuraman, S. V. (1976). The urban informal sector: Concept, measurement and policy. *International Labour Review*, *114*(1), 69–81.

Sethuraman, S. V. (1981). *The urban informal sector in developing countries: Employment poverty and environment*. International Labor Organization, Geneva.

132   References

Siddiki, J. (2014). *The size and development of the shadow economy in Bangladesh: An empirical investigation* (No. 3). Faculty of Arts and Social Sciences, Kingston University, London.

Siddiqi, M. N. (2006). Islamic banking and finance in theory and practice: A survey of state of the art. *Islamic Economic Studies, 13*(2), 1–48.

Sindzingre, A. (2006). The relevance of the concepts of formality and informality: A theoretical appraisal. In *Linking the formal and informal economy: Concepts and policies.* Oxford University Press, Oxford.

Singh, A., Jain-Chandra, S., & Mohommad, A. (2012). *Inclusive growth, institutions, and the underground economy* (No. 12/47). International Monetary Fund, Washington, DC.

Smith, P. (1994). *Assessing the size of the underground economy: The statistics Canada perspectives.* Canadian Economic Observer, Catalogue No. 11-010,3.16-33, at 3.18 Spiro.

Smith, S. P. (1976). Pay differentials between federal government and private sector workers. *ILR Review, 29*(2), 179–197.

Sookram, S., & Watson, P. K. (2008). Small-business participation in the informal sector of an emerging economy. *The Journal of Development Studies, 44*(10), 1531–1553.

Spiro, P. S. (1993). Evidence of a post-GST increase in the underground economy. *Canadian Tax Journal/Revue Fiscale Canadienne, 41*(2), 247–258.

Stănculescu, M. (2005). Working conditions in the informal sector. *SEER: Journal for Labour and Social Affairs in Eastern Europe, 8*(3), 79–93.

Standing, G. (1999). Global feminization through flexible labor: A theme revisited. *World Development, 27*(3), 583–602.

Swaminathan, M. (1991). *Understanding the "informal sector": A survey.* World Institute for Development Economics Research of the United Nations University (No, 95). Massachusetts: Centre for International Studies, MIT.

Tan, Y. L., Habibullah, M. S., & Yiew, T. H. (2016). The shadow economy in Malaysia: Evidence from an ARDL model. *International Journal of Economics & Management, 10*(2), 161–277.

Tanzi, V. (1980). The underground economy in the United States: Estimates and implications. *PSL Quarterly Review, 33*(135).

Tanzi, V. (1999). Uses and abuses of estimates of the underground economy. *The Economic Journal, 109*(456), 338–347.

Tedds, L. (2005). *The underground economy in Canada* (No. 4229). Available at ProQuest Database.

Teilhet-Waldorf, S., & Waldorf, W. H. (1983). Earnings of self-employed in an informal sector: A case study of Bangkok. *Economic Development and Cultural Change, 31*(3), 587–607.

Thomas, J. (1992). *Informal economic activity.* Harvester Wheatsheaf, London.

Thompson, N. M. (2009). Why the Hawkers are back on the Pavement [online]. *Accra.* Available at http://news.myjoyonline.com/features/200907/33352.asp.

Tokman, V. E. (1978). An exploration into the nature of informal – Formal sector relationships. *World Development, 6*(10), 1065–1075.

Tokman, V. E. (1989). Policies for a heterogeneous informal sector in Latin America. *World Development, 17*(7), 1067–1076.

Tokman, V. E. (2001). Integrating the informal sector in the modernization process. *SAIS Review, 21*(1), 45–60.

Torgler, B., & Schneider, F. (2007). *Shadow economy, tax morale, governance and institutional quality: A panel analysis* (No. 210). School of Economics and Finance, Queensland University of Technology, Queensland.

Torgler, B., Schneider, F., & Schaltegger, C. A. (2010). Local autonomy, tax morale, and the shadow economy. *Public Choice, 144*(1), 293–321.

References 133

Trebicka, B. (2014). MIMIC model: A tool to estimate the shadow economy. *Academic Journal of Interdisciplinary Studies*, 3(6), 295.

Tucker, M. (1982). The underground economy in Australia. *The Underground Economy in the United States and Abroad*, 315–322.

United Nations Economic Commission for Europe. (1993). *System of national accounts*. United Nations, Washington, DC.

Voicu, C. (2012). Economics and 'underground' economy theory. *Theoretical and Applied Economics*, 7(7), 71.

Walker, T. W., & Wade, C. J. (2011). *Nicaragua: Living in the shadow of the eagle*. Westview Press, Westview.

Walsh, A. C. (1982). *Migration, urbanization and development in South Pacific countries*. Comparative Study on Migration, Urbanization and Development in the SCAP Region (No. 6). United Nations, New York.

Warde, I. (2000). *Islamic finance in the global economy*. Edinburgh University Press, Edinburgh.

WIEGO. (2011). *The informal economy debate: Four dominant schools of thought*. Available at www.wiego.org/informal-economy-debate-four-schools.

Williams, C. C. (2004). *Cash-in-hand work: The underground sector and the hidden economy of favours*. Palgrave Macmillan, Basingstoke.

Williams, C. C. (2005). *A commodified world: Mapping the limits of capitalism*. Zed Books, London.

Williams, C. C. (2006). Evaluating the magnitude of the shadow economy: A direct survey approach. *Journal of Economic Studies*, 33(5), 369–385.

Williams, C. C. (2007). The nature of entrepreneurship in the informal sector: Evidence from England. *Journal of Developmental Entrepreneurship*, 12(02), 239–254.

Williams, C. C. (2008). *The hidden enterprise culture: Entrepreneurship in the underground economy*. Edward Elgar, Cheltenham.

Williams, C. C. (2014). Out of the shadows: A classification of economies by the size and character of their informal sector. *Work, Employment and Society*, 28(5), 735–753.

Williams, C. C., & Nadin, S. (2010). Entrepreneurship and the informal economy: An overview. *Journal of Developmental Entrepreneurship*, 15(4), 361–378.

Williams, C. C., & Round, J. (2008). A critical evaluation of romantic depictions of the informal economy. *Review of Social Economy*, 66(3), 297–323.

Williams, C.C., & Round, J. (2009), Evaluating informal entrepreneurs' motives: Some lessons from Moscow. *International Journal of Entrepreneurial Behaviour and Research*, 15(1), 94–107.

Williams, C. C., Round, J., & Rodgers, P. (2006). Beyond necessity-and opportunity-driven entrepreneurship: Some case study evidence from Ukraine. *Journal of Business and Entrepreneurship*, 18(2), 22.

Williams, C. C., Round, J., & Rodgers, P. (2013). *The role of informal economies in the post-Soviet world: The end of transition?* Routledge, London.

Williams, C. C., & Shahid, M. S. (2016). Informal entrepreneurship and institutional theory: Explaining the varying degrees of (in) formalization of entrepreneurs in Pakistan. *Entrepreneurship & Regional Development*, 28(2), 1–25.

Williams, C. C., & Windebank, J. (2003). *Poverty and the third way*. Routledge, London.

Willis, R. J., & Rosen, S. (1979). Education and self-selection. *Journal of Political Economy*, 87(5), 7–36.

Willman-Navarro, A. (2008). Informal economy. *International Encyclopedia of Public Policy – Governance in a Global Age*, 4, 369–381.

134 *References*

Windmeijer, F. (2005). A finite sample correction for the variance of linear efficient two-step GMM estimators. *Journal of Econometrics, 126*(1), 25–51.

Young, K., & Moser, C. (1981). Women and the informal sector. *Institute of Development Studies Bulletin, 12*(3), 54–62.

Yusoff, M. (2006). Fiscal policy in an Islamic economy and the role of Zakat. *IIUM Journal of Economics and Management, 14*(2), 117–145.

Index

Page locators in **bold** indicate a table. Page locators in *italics* indicate a figure.

Abdih, Yasser 66, 83
accuracy 18–19, 28, 40, 104
Adam, M.C. 35
administrative 9, 30
aggregate demand (AD) 20, 33, 36
agreement: contractual 3, 21, 47; informal 45
Albu, Lucian Liviu 37
allocation of resources 25, 84, 102, 106
Anderson, Theodore Wilbur 70
appendices 107
AR. *see* autoregressive
Arby, Muhammad (*et al* 2010) 37
Arellano, Manuel 70–73
Arias, Omar 36
Arvate, Paulo 37, 64, 66, 74
Asiedu, Edward 37
authenticity 18, 28, 40, 104
automated teller machines (ATMs) 67, 75, 77, 94, **101**
autoregressive (AR) 71–72
autoregressivedistributed lag (ARDL) 37–38
Aytemiz, L 38, 65–66

bad government 51
Bagachwa, Mboya S.D. 12
Baltagi, Badi H. (*et al* 2005) 69
Banerjee, Biswajit 44
Başar, Remzi 20
Baxter, Michael W.P. 44
Bayar, Yilmaz 38, 65–66, 86
bazaar sector 43
Beavon, Keith 44
Beck, Thorsten 64–66, 74
Becker, Kristina Flodman 36
Benería, Lourdes 52
Berdiev, Aziz N. 38–39, 64–65, 84, 86

Bhattacharyya, Dilip K. 12
Birkbeck, Chris 44–45
Bittencourt, Manoel (*et al* 2014) 39, 67
black market 20–21, 55–56, 60
black underground 55
Blackburn, Keith (*et al* 2012) 38
Blundell, Richard 71
Boeke, J.H. 5
Bojnec, Štefan 39
Bolnick, Bruce R. 44
Bond, Stephen 70–73
Bose, Niloy (*et al* 2012) 38
Bourhaba, Othmane 37
Bover, Olympia 71–72
Bovi, Maurizio 19
bribery 13, 30, 51
Bromley, Ray 44
business: activities 43, 51; financing 56–57, 60; freedom (LBF) 64, 79, **117**; models 25, 50; opportunities 43, 53; registration and documentation 36, 45–46, 48, 56, 60

Cagan, Phillip 7
Capasso, Salvatore 38, 40, 65
capitalist: era 3; production 3, 45
Carter, Michael 12
Castells, Manuel 47, 52
Cebula, Richard J. 29
Chaudhuri, Kausik (*et al* 2006) 37
circuits, upper/lower 44–45
COMCEC. *see* Standing Committee for Economic and Commercial Cooperation of the Organisation of the Islamic Cooperative
commodity production, petty 3, 45
community, impact on 4

136 *Index*

competition: creation of 33, 54, 57; unfair 19, 53, 106
complementary theory 42, 52, 60–61
consumption 22–23, 74, 78, 84
control: government 4; variables 65, 67–68, 75, 83
correlation analysis 79, **80**, 94
corruption 8, 18, 30, 37, 60
credit market 40
criminal activities 7, 12, 15, 55–56, 60, 62
Cumming, Douglas J. (*et al* 2014) 76
currency demand 37, 74

Dabla-Norris, Era (*et al 2008)* 39
Dannhaeuser, Norbert 44
De Koker, Louis 40
De Soto, Hernando 48–49
Dell'Anno, Roberto 15, 19, 35, 65–67, 74–75, 83, 101–101
demand, supply and 49
democracy 49, 51
deregulation 39
descriptive statistics 77, **78**
development: financial (*see* financial development); monetary 38
Din, Badariah H (*et al* 2016) 38, 65–67
Djankov, Simeon (*et al* 2002) 38
Dreher, Axel (*et al* 2009) 66, 83
drug dealing/manufacturing 15, 23
Dualist school 42, 48, 58–59, 61, 83, 102

economic activities: in shadow economy 2, 4, 6, 8–9, 15, 33, 36; variables and 28, 40, 104
Economic Development with Unlimited Supplies of Labour (Lewis) 2
economic freedom (LECOF) variable 63, 74, 77
economic growth: effects of 83; stages of 36, 43
economic policies: development of 19; effective 18, 28, 40, 104
Eilat, Yair 35
Ela, Mehmet 34, 67, 74
Elbahnasawy, Nasr (*et al* 2016) 84
Elgin, Ceyhun 38, 64, 67, 74
employment: full 3, 47–48; informal 3, 40; opportunities 33, 43, 83
entrepreneurs 9, 27, 54, 59–61, 64, 106
estimating models 63
estimation equations: determinants of shadow economy 63; financial development 65; financial inclusion 67

estimations, method of 68
European Union (EU) 38

Farazi, Subika 40
Faspareniene, Ligita 66–67, 84
favoritism 51
Fedotenkov, Igor 102
Feige, Edgar L. 5, 8
Feld, Lars 18
financial development: estimation equations 65–67, 76; impacts of 35, 38, 63, 77
financial exclusion 23, 27, 75, 106
financial inclusion: effect of 68, 76, 86; impact of 67–68, 86–87; influence of 86
financial institutions: role of 26 *see also* Islamic micro financial institutions
firm centered sector 43
fixed effect (FE) 70, **81**, *see also* Appendices
formal (industrial) sector 3, 24, 33, 46, 53, 60, 74
formal economy: cost of labor 29, 67; employers in 52; impact on 2, 4, 16; isolation from 42; participation in 32
fraud 13, **15**, 23, 26
free market 4, 20, 22, 39
Frey, Bruno S. 19, 32, 35
Friedman, Eric (*et al* 2000) 18, 30, 32
Friedman, Milton 20–21
Fuest, Clemens 19
Furnivall, John S. 2, 5

gambling **15**, 23–24
Gatti, Roberta 39
Gaysset, Isabelle 76
Geertz, Clifford 43–44
generalized method of movements (GMM) 38, 69–73; estimators 71–72
Gerry, Chris 44
Ghana, economy of 1–3, 5, 37
Giles, David E.A. 30, 35, 84
Ginsburgh, Victor 35
GMM. *see* generalized method movements
Gobbi, Giorgio 40
goods and services: cost/pricing of 20, 43, 46; production of 12–13, 44, 55; public 11, 32, 36; shadow market for 2, 5
government: dissatisfaction with 2, 30; expenditure 18, 55, 64, 74, 83; intervention 3, 49, 51; statistics 5–6, 20
green economy 57
gross domestic product (GDP) 6, 9, 12, *13*, 24, 37, 67; bank deposits to 67–68, 75, **101**

Index 137

Guibourg, Gabriela 5
Gulzer, Ahmed (*et al* 2010) 30

Hart, Keith 1–5, 7, 19, 28, 44, 104
Hassan, Mai 37, 64–67, 74, 84
high income OIC countries (HOIC) 9
Hill, Rod 29
Honorati, Maddalena 39
Hoseini, Mohammad 64–66, 74
Hosseini, Abdollah (*et al* 2014) 38
Hsiao, Cheng 70

illegal activities 8, **15**, 23, 56, 60–62
Illegalist theory 55, 62
ILO. *see* International Finance Corporation
Imanoglu, Hatice 38
inclusionist perspective 42, 56
income inequality 31, 44, 46, 52
industrialization 3, 5, 43, 46, 69
informal sector 5–8, 19–20, 25–27, 45–46
informality 5, 49
instrumental variable 70–71
International Finance Corporation (IFC) 39
International Labor Organization (ILO) 1,
    3–5, 7, 19, 28, 44, 52, 104
International Monetary Fund (IMF) 4, 55,
    73, 76
Islamic banking 26, 47
Islamic economic system 22–23
Islamic finance 24–27, 61
Islamic financial institutions (IFIs) 25
Islamic finance corporation (IFC) 39
Islamic micro financial institutions (IMFI)
    26, 61

Jagannathan, N. Vihay 45
Jappelli, Tullio 38, 40, 65
Jellinek, L. 44
Jentzsch, Nicola 40
Johnson, Betty J. 30
Johnson, Simon (*et al* 1997/1998b) 30, 32
Joo, Donghun 30–31
Jourdain, Robert 44

Kabir, Muhammed 29
Kaliberda, Aleksander 35
Kaplinsky, Raphael 44
Karlinger, Liliane 16
Kaufmann, Daniel 35
Kenya 1, 5, 7
Keynes, Milton 3
Khamis, Melanie 36
Kim, Dai-Won (*et al* 2018) 76, 87, 103
King, Kenneth J. 44

La Porta, Rafael 39
Langdon, Steven 44
Law, Siong Hook 74
Legalist/neoliberal School 21, 36, 48,
    50–51, 61
Lemieux, Thomas (*et al* 1994) 31
Levenson, Alec R. 44–45
Lewis, W. Arthur 3–5
liberalization 37
Lucinda, Claudio 37, 64, 66, 74

macroeconomic: fundamentals 1, 19, 82;
    variables 18–19, 28, 40, 104–105
Mahmoudzadeh, Mahmoud (*et al* 2017)
    64–66, 74
Maki, Daiki 38, 65
Maloney, William F. 44–45
Mama, Hammida 37
Marinov, Anton 30
Marx, Karl 3, 5
Mazumdar, Dipak 44
McGee, T.G. (*et al* 1980) 44
Medina, Leandro 9, 63, 66, 74, 83
medium, micro, and small businesses
    (MMSEs) 39
Merrick, Thomas W. 44
MIMIC. *see* multiple indicators, multiple
    cause model
mixed economies 52
mode of production 44–45
modern perspective 42, 57, 62
Monte Carlo study 71
Moser, Caroline 44
movement conditions 70–71
multiple indicators, multiple cause model
    18, 37, 74

Nastav, Bojan 39
Nattress, Nicoli Jean (1987) 45
Neaime, Simon 76
Newwirth, Robert 37
Nihan, Georges (*et al* 1979) 44
Nikopour, Hesam 13
Norcliffe, glen 44

OECD (Organisation for Economic
    Co-operation and Development) 16, 18, 35
official sector 20, 23–25, 27, 33, 37
official economy 2, *16*, 33
Onnis, Luisanna 64, 83
Organisation of Islamic Cooperation
    (OIC): member states 5, 36, 76;
    non-OIC countries, comparisons 11, 66,
    85, 87, 92, 94

138   Index

Orviská, Marta (*et al* 2006) 16
Ott, Katarina 30, 33, 35
Ouédraogo, Idrissa M. 67
Ozturk, Omer Faruk 65–66, 86

Peattie, Lisa R. 52
petty commodity production 45
Pissarides, Christopher 7
policy implications 104
policy makers 2, 18, 53, 105
Portes, Alejandro 5, 47, 50, 52
postcolonial 50–51, 56–57
private sector, domestic credit to 65, 75,
   77, 79, 85, **101**
privatization 39
pro-poor urban planning 57, 61
prostitution **15**, 23
Provisional Contribution on Financial
   Transactions (CPMF) 37
public sector services 29, 32

regulations: excessive 18, 28, 40, 49,
   104–105; government 7, 19, 21, 30, 50,
   54; intensity of 31
Remeikiene, Rita 64, 66–67, 84
Riedel, Nadine 18
Rogerson, Christian 44
Roodman, David 72–73
Round, John 50

Santos, Milton 44–45
Saraç, Mehmet 20
Sargan, J. Denis 73
Sassen-Koob, Saskia 47
Saunoris, James 38–39, 65, 84, 86
Schaefer, Kathleen K. 49
Schneider, Friedrich: informal economy,
   size of 30; shadow economy, background
   of 1, 5, 8–9, 13, 16, 19, 32–33
sector: economic 7; formal (*see* formal
   sector); informal (*see* informal sector);
   official (*see* official sector); private (*see*
   private sector); traditional 3
Segendorf, Björn 5
Sethuraman, S.V. 43
shadow economy: activities 6, 8–9, 15, 19,
   33, 36; background 1; cycle (vicious)
   of *12*, 32; definitions and meanings
   6, 9, *16*, 39; determinants of 35, 63,
   81–82; distribution **15**, 15–16, *17*, 20,
   22; historical development of 2, 104;
   interest in 2, 22; measurements of 9, 11;
   monetary/nonmonetary activities13, **15**

see also development, monetary; sample/
   subsample 79; sector of 1–3, 5, 7, **15**, 19,
   23; size of *10*, *11*, *13*, *14*; sophisticated
   nature of 28–29, 59, 104; tax bypass/
   evasion 8–9, 13, 16; theories 42, 59;
   unjust distribution of resources 20
Shleifer, Andrei 39
Siddiki, Jalal 37
Singh, Anoop (*et al* 2012) 67
Singh, Nirvikar 74
skill development 44, 46
Smith, Adam 53
Smith, Phillip 12
smuggling 8, 13, **15**, 23
social security system 20, 53–55
social security contribution 29–31
Sookram, Sandra 31
Spiro, Peter S. 30
Standing Committee for Economic
   and Commercial Cooperation of the
   Organisation of the Islamic Cooperative
   (COMCEC) 5
Stengos, Thanasis 37
stolen goods **15**, 23
structuralist/dependency school 47
supply chain 46, 60

Takaful 26–27
Tan, Yan-Ling (*et al* 2016) 37
taxation 29, 32, 53–54, 60, 74
taxes, evade 13, 16, 21, 39, 53, 57
Tedds, Lindsay M. 35, 84
Teilhet-Waldorf, Saral 44
Theory of Economic Growth (Lewis) 2
Tirelli, Patrizio 64, 83
Torgler, Benno (*et al* 2010) 30, 84

underground: economy 8, 12, 16;
   production 55–56
unemployment 33
United Nation Government Revenue
   Dataset 2017 73–74
United Nations Economic Commission for
   Europe 55
unlawful agents 55–56
Uras, Burak R. 38, 64, 67, 74

variables: comparative mean **102**;
   correlation coefficients **80**; description
   of 73–74; macroeconomic 18–19, 28,
   40, 104–105; measure of institutional
   101
Voluntarist/Rational Exit theory 53

Index 139

Waldorf, W.H. 44
Walsh, A.C. 44
Watson, Patrick Kent 31
Weber, Guglielmo 7
Weck-Hanneman, Hannelore 35
Williams, Colin C. 50, 52
Willman-Navarro, Alys 3
Windmeijer, Frank 72–73
Word Development Indicator (WDI) 73
World Bank 4, 7, 39, 59, 75–76

World Governance Indicator (WGI) 73
World Heritage Foundation (WHF) 73
World War II 4–5

Xtabond2 73

Young, Kate 44

Zinnes, Clifford 35
Zizza, Roberta 40

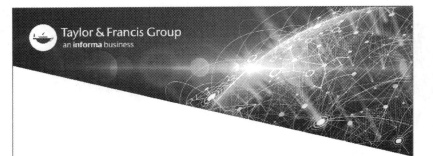

Printed in the United States
by Baker & Taylor Publisher Services